At the End of the Storm
There's a Golden Sky

To The lucky
Winner in the Raffle

Best Wishes
From the author !!!

JFT 97

YNWA

At the End of the Storm There's a Golden Sky

by

Christopher Whittle

FIRST EDITION

Paperback ISBN: 978-1-80227-889-7
eBook ISBN: 978-1-80227-586-5

Table of Contents

The 97 Angels

John Alfred Anderson 62
Colin Mark Ashcroft 19
James Gary Aspinall 18
Kester Roger Marcus Ball 16
Gerard Bernard Patrick Baron 67
Simon Bell 17
Barry Sidney Bennett 26
David John Benson 22
David William Birtle 22
Tony Bland 22
Paul David Brady 21
Andrew Mark Brookes 26
Carl Brown 18
David Steven Brown 25
Henry Thomas Burke 47
Peter Andrew Burkett 24
Paul William Carlile 19
Raymond Thomas Chapman 50
Gary Christopher Church 19
Joseph Clark 29
Paul Clark 18
Gary Collins 22
Stephen Paul Copoc 20
Tracey Elizabeth Cox 23

James Phillip Delaney 19
Andrew Devine 22 (55)
Christopher Barry Devonside 18
Christopher Edwards 29
Vincent Michael Fitzsimmons 34
Thomas Steven Fox 21
Jon-Paul Gilhooley 10
Barry Glover 27
Ian Thomas Glover 20
Derrick George Godwin 24
Roy Harry Hamilton 34
Philip Hammond 14
Eric Hankin 33
Garry Harrison 27
Stephen Francis Hamilton 31
Peter Andrew Harrison 15
David Hawley 39
James Robert Hennessy 29
Paul Anthony Hewitson 26
Carl Darren Hewitt 17
Nicholas Michael Hewitt 16
Sarah Louise Hicks 19
Victoria Jane Hicks 15
Gordon Rodney Horn 20
Arthur Horrocks 41
Thomas Howard 39
Thomas Anthony Howard 14
Eric George Hughes 41
Alan Johnston 29
Christine Anne Jones 27

Gary Philip Jones 18
Richard Jones 25
Nicholas Peter Joynes 27
Anthony Peter Kelly 29
Michael David Kelly 38
Carl David Lewis 18
David William Mather 19
Brian Christopher Matthews 38
Francis Joseph MacAllister 27
John McBrien 18
Marian Hazel McCabe 21
Joseph Daniel McCarthy 21
Peter McDonnell 21
Alan McGlone 28
Keith McGrath 17
Paul Brian Murray 14
Lee Nicol 14
Stephen Francis O'Neill 17
Jonathon Owens 18
William Roy Pemberton 23
Carl William Rimmer 21
David George Rimmer 38
Graham John Roberts 24
Steven Joseph Robinson 17
Henry Charles Rogers 17
Andrew Sefton 23
Inger Shah 35
Paula Ann Smith 26
Adam Edward Spearitt 14
Philip John Steele 15

David Leonard Thomas 23
Patrick John Thompson 35
Peter Reuben Thompson 30
Stuart Paul William Thompson 17
Peter Francis Tootle 21
Christopher James Traynor 26
Kevin Martin Traynor 16
Kevin Tyrell 15
Colin Wafer 19
Ian David Whelan 19
Martin Kevin Wild 29
Kevin Daniel Williams 15
Graham John Wright 17

YNWA GBNF JFT97

Preface

This is my second 'Hillsborough' book. My first attempt at writing was as a novice. I readily admit that it was a bit rough around the edges, so to speak. A few glaring errors kind of stopped it being a good book.

You know what they say, 'Pride comes before a fall'. Well, my stupid pride got in the way and anger and frustration enveloped me. That is what PTSD does to you. My all-encompassing rage lost many friends along the way.

I had to withdraw from social media, really to keep my sanity. There were a lot of issues going on, some of them self-inflicted and some not. It has been a rollercoaster over the past few years without a doubt. I have lost both my parents over the past nine years. My dad passed away on 8th November 2013 from cancer of the gallbladder. He died peacefully with his loving family by his side at Dove Court Nursing Home. This was tempered by the birth of my beloved granddaughter, the beautiful Monica Rose. My little princess. She was born on 17th December 2013, a few short weeks after the loss of my dad.

I lost my mum, just less than two years ago, on 6th March 2020. She had a long battle with dementia. As with my dad, my mum passed away in Dove Court Nursing Home. This was a devastating time in our lives, in our family. The past few years have been horrific personally, when my own health came into question after a series of serious conditions and a long stint in hospital. There will be more on this later.

I have missed so much football and my beloved Liverpool during my health crisis. I have missed European Cup glory and our sixth title. I have missed our nineteenth league championship, or most of it. Our thirty-year wait is over.

We did it for the 97.

YNWA

Christopher Whittle
January 2022

Chapter One

The Killing Fields
of Leppings Lane

In my first and previous book, *With Hope in My Heart*, I wrote about the horrific tragedy of Hillsborough, when on a sunny, warm, spring afternoon, 97 innocent men, women and children were unlawfully killed. Hillsborough was the worst sporting disaster in British history. It was a disaster that was controversial, devastating, horrific and disturbing. On a worldwide scale, one of the worst disasters ever witnessed.

Yet, Hillsborough was different to any other tragedy. That is not belittling other disasters, far from it. Any disaster is a tragedy and I feel for those who lost their lives, the survivors and the bereaved.

So, why was Hillsborough different?

Not only did people shockingly lose their lives along with survivors who tried to save their own lives and the lives of others in a sea of turmoil, death and horror, they also had to contend with falsehood, lies, collusion, fabrication and vile myths. Those selfless heroes who did the job of the emergency services, rescuing the injured and the dying, using advertising hoardings as makeshift stretchers, amidst the chaos of the killing fields of Leppings Lane.

I wrote in graphic detail of that horrific, mind-blowing day that changed my life, and the lives of my fellow survivors, and the bereaved families, in the first book. As I stated back then, it was a very difficult, mind-numbing experience to write about. Something so unbearable, so shocking, it is a very difficult thing to contemplate, never mind put into words. Yet, on the other hand, reliving it all was essentially cathartic. It was something I really had to do. I would say it was part of the healing process.

So, what happened that day, 15th April 1989?

Like many others have talked about, it was a bright, warm, sunny spring day. It was a perfect day. Everything seemed peaceful as we travelled to Sheffield, looking forward to another FA Cup semi-final. The same ground, the same opponents and hopefully the same result. It was a hard fought 2-1 victory in 1988. I do remember the situation in the ground, in the same Leppings Lane end. I also remember the filtering system that was operated by the police. You were told to show your ticket in order to be able to gain access to the concourse. The bizzies (police) were pleasant enough and courteous. I spent time sitting on a wall by the river which ran alongside the stadium. I sipped a couple of beers and read the match day programme. It was a pleasurable early afternoon. It was fairly easy to get through the turnstiles, around 2 p.m. The one thing I remember in 1988 was the fact that the entrance to the tunnel was closed or sealed off. There was no option but to go to the side pens. I recall being in Pen 1.

As the kick off approached, it became increasingly uncomfortable in the pen. There were some minor injuries and the like. It was a struggle in there, and I was quite relieved when the game ended, with a 2-1 victory for the Reds. I caught a special bus back into Sheffield and the train home.

And so, to 15th April 1989, when 97 innocent men, women and children went to a football match and never came home. The cause of death was termed as 'traumatic or compression asphyxiation' in virtually all of the cases. That is not in doubt. What is in doubt, was the supposed time of death. A uniform cut off point of 3:15 p.m. and the ludicrous notion by the then South Yorkshire coroner, Stefan Popper, that all of the then 96 victims were dead by the time stated. This proved to be wholly controversial and an absolute pack of lies. There were many lies told that day, and many years beyond. It was a convenient lie to brush things under the carpet and pin the blame on the brave fans. Unfortunately for them, we would not accept the vicious lies. Forgive the sporting analogy, but we would not play ball. Yet, it would take over a quarter of a century to expose the lies, the cover up, the fabrication, the coercion, the myths, the bullying, the mud-slinging and the corruption of those at fault, and those connected to it. Luckily, there was a resolute, tough, brave and unbreakable set of people who would not accept defeat, who would question everything that needed to be questioned, and would never give up. I am talking, of course, about the amazing, bereaved families and the heroic, brave survivors. There are some that we have lost over the years, as time passed on and health problems affected them. For this, I salute them all.

When you are part of a strong and uncompromising group of people, you are going to have disagreements and arguments along the way. It is totally natural. On a personal level, I can relate to that and readily say that I did things I am not proud of. I let anger get in the way that ultimately destroyed friendships and that is something which I deeply regret. Therefore, I publicly, and without reservation, offer my wholehearted and deeply meaningful apology, from the bottom of my heart.

I have often been asked what was it like? How did you feel? Were you injured?

That is a very complex thing to talk about and it would mean I would have to go deep into my psyche, and face the depths of hell. Naturally, it was hell. Hell on Earth. I do not know if you ever saw the excellent and extremely shocking war film, *The Killing Fields*. It was based in Cambodia in the early 1970s and was the true and very harrowing story revolving around an American journalist, who was covering the war and the atrocities of the regime, and, of course, the infamous dictator, Pol Pot. The journalist involved struck up a friendship with a local guide and the film revolves around them. It was a remarkable piece of cinema that won a number of Oscars. If you could get to see it, please do so, it is very worthwhile and extremely thought-provoking. Hillsborough was our killing field. The needless loss of life, a massive cover up, blatant lies and the sickening way in which those who lost their lives, the survivors and the bereaved families were shockingly treated. Yet, things never seem to change. If you look at the long list of miscarriages of justice, what is evident, and as clear as day, is the fact that protected self-interests, massive cover ups, and the absolute denial of justice still holds sway, even now. This is very true in regards to Hillsborough, and other notable and controversial cases including Lockerbie, Stephen Lawrence, Damilola Taylor, Grenfell, Bloody Sunday, the Birmingham Six, the Guildford Four, and others. The common link is the innocent being let down by the corrupt system, and having to fight year after year, and decade after decade, to get to the truth. It is perfectly true that justice delayed is justice denied.

I wish to return to the horrific scenes that I encountered on Saturday 15th April 1989. This is something that I omitted, in the most part, in the original book due to the graphic nature that I witnessed on the pitch and the scenes of absolute carnage. In the first book, I explained about the crush outside Leppings Lane and the dark tunnel which led to the central pens—Pen 3 and Pen 4—and my personal recollections of trying to survive, and fight for my own life, in the intense vice-like crush in Pen 4. After I got through the vicious and claustrophobic heat, and the airless, dark tunnel with its uncompromising 1:6 gradient, I found myself in front of the barrier directly by the tunnel itself, just a few short feet away. Naturally, as the crush developed and intensified, the vice tightened and my chest hit the cold steel with a tremendous and violent surge. I screamed out in absolute pain and agony, as I tried to gain a few inches of relief, but it was impossible to do so. I was totally breathless, my chest expanding, ribs intensely hurting, my life flashing before me, as the intense heat enveloped me. I was feeling faint, ready to pass out. My legs were like two tubs of jelly. I was giving up. I was going under, almost to certain death. At that moment, my knees buckled and down I went. If I had stayed down, I know I would have lost my life. Yet, it was one of those moments. My moment. My guardian angel moment. I was pulled up on my feet. I was told by this stranger in red that, and I quote: 'You are not going to die, not today.'

Those words have stayed with me for more than thirty years. In a way, they have haunted me. After I got my bearings, the guy had gone. I had not seen him before, or since. I just fervently hope that he was not one of the 97. I just do not know.

My breathing was shallow, and my ribs and chest hurt like hell. I had to focus to get out of that horrific pen. All I could smell was a vile, sickening stench. The smell of death. Much death. Uncompromising and agonising death. The same medical terminology was used time and again: traumatic or compression asphyxiation. Not a very pleasant scenario, believe me. The intense crushing, followed by difficulty in breathing, and finally brain damage. The colour of the skin is blue and purple. Death comes within a period of up to half an hour, though this can vary depending on the patient. This totally refutes and dismisses Popper's claims that all those who died, did so by 3:15 p.m. This was a convenient lie, all part of the cover up orchestrated by the coroner, Stefan Popper. Yet, not everyone complied to this. This was challenged by bereaved families. Most notably, of course, by the wonderful Anne Williams, the real Iron Lady.

More than a quarter of a century passed by before there was some kind of justice. There will be more on this later.

Chapter Two

Undignified Death

When you lose someone in such horrific circumstances, such as at Hillsborough, you would expect to be provided with common decency, sympathetic respect, courtesy, empathy, understanding and compassion. That was not the case following Hillsborough. Instead, the bereaved families were treated with suspicion, doubt, crass indignation, accusations and odious criticism. Can you imagine if that was you? How would you feel? What happened on that night was the most callous series of events that was shocking beyond reason, and vile to the very extreme.

The very distressing identification process was one which was beyond any degree of decency. This took place inside the club gymnasium at Hillsborough, where almost 100 men, women and children were crushed to death. The actual cause of death was traumatic or compression asphyxiation. So, what is traumatic or compression asphyxiation?

Traumatic or compression asphyxiation develops due to a compression of the thoracic cavity. Such compression of the chest can result in severe breathing difficulties and heart failure, as well as extensive brain injury or damage. This is relevant to crushing, such as at Hillsborough, when so many people lost their lives that afternoon.

A few hours later, the relatives came, in deep and unbearable shock. They were told to go to the gymnasium at Hillsborough. Some came on coaches whilst others came independently in cars. Earlier in the day, some relatives had frantically searched the two main hospitals—the Northern General and the Royal Hallamshire—which were set up for the emergency response and port of call for the already distressed and traumatised relatives. What transpired were scenes of chaos, confusion and absolute turmoil. You would expect some kind of compassion and reassurance from the so-called 'health professionals'. Not relatively so. There were doctors, nurses, paramedics who were genuinely sympathetic, caring and showed empathy. However, there were those that were not. In the identification process at the gymnasium, it was all about accusations, interrogation, pouring scorn that was acid-like. There were vile smears, confrontation and absolutely zero respect. The whole process was flawed, and of no feeling whatsoever. Whether it was the herding of the already distressed and grieving relatives to the gymnasium, the pinned Polaroid photos of the dead in an horrific state, the chaotic scenes of seemingly endless body bags, the uncaring nature of identification as the green coloured body bags were slowly unzipped to reveal the pained, disfigured faces of blue and purple, or the abject horror and terror of the loved ones having to face the shocking process of identification. Imagine the sickening thought of your loved one being identified in a most callous, vile, shocking way. Added to this was the forceful interpretation that was demanded by officialdom, as bereaved and distraught families tried desperately to hold them, kiss them, hug them. The crass insistence of 'no touching', and the wicked statement repeatedly argued that, 'the body belongs to the coroner of South Yorkshire, not you'.

Stunningly awful and without reason, that totally and morally abused every single human right. I often remember the words spoken by my late father, 'That was man's inhumanity to man', when he referred to the Holocaust, Auschwitz and the death camps, during the Final Solution. Well, this was South Yorkshire's Holocaust, their Auschwitz, their death camp and their Final Solution. You may think this to be harsh, and close to the knuckle, and a certain graphic intensity, but this was real. Shockingly real.

Then came the blood alcohol tests on those who died. Shockingly, this included young children. The narrative was that the police, the coroner, and others would use this to cement their case that would revolve around drunkenness, ticketless fans and violent crowd disorder. The false accusations would stick, and Popper was perfectly happy with this scenario. Despite the fact there was no evidence, that drinking was not a major issue, that ticketless fans were not to blame. The HSE (Health and Safety Executive) would prove this with their own investigations. As for violent disorder, nobody had any desire to fight as the tragedy unfolded, as they were too busy trying to live and survive, helping the injured and dying, or frantically trying to find loved ones or friends. The crazy notion that violent thugs caused Hillsborough is an absolute outrage. It was more to do with finding convenient scapegoats, and preserve vested self-interests and their fat pensions.

Chapter Three

Rewriting Hillsborough: Lies, Murdoch, Mackenzie and the S*N

A few days after Hillsborough, the city of Liverpool, even the whole country, were in a deep state of shock. At that time, a total of 93 men, women and children were dead just for attending a football match. This would rise to 95. Eventually, a few years later, the final total rose to 96 after the family of Tony Bland took the agonising decision to turn off his life support at Airedale Hospital, near Keighley in West Yorkshire. Tony had been in PVS or persistent vegetative state ever since the fatal crush. Now, the figure has reached 97, following the death earlier this year of Andrew Devine, a remarkable man who lived for more than thirty years. A true hero and an inspiration.

Those few days that followed the tragedy at Hillsborough, plans were afoot to rewrite Hillsborough. A story had developed from White's News Agency in Sheffield, around secretive meetings with South Yorkshire Police Federation rep, one Paul Middup. The absolute lies spoken centred on drunkenness, ticketless fans and forced entry. That was the mere start as more vile and wicked accusations were centred at the Liverpool fans and the blatant lies of 'urinating on brave cops', 'robbing the dead' etc. Of course, it did not take long for the gutter rag to make hay. This was the perfect opportunity for those involved, either directly or indirectly, to pursue a false narrative which would carry on for more than a quarter of a century.

Tuesday 18th April 1989 is a date that can never be forgotten. *That* headline of 'The Truth', of course, can never be forgiven. The crass headline was the dirty work of Kelvin Mackenzie, a man still universally hated in Liverpool. The fact is Mackenzie wanted to use an even more unpalatable headline, 'You Scum'. These were the kind of odious individuals who we had to deal with. With the rabid right-wing Tory press, their illicit paymaster, Rupert Murdoch, and the sordid connections with Thatcher and her cronies, it is plain to see the very strong link of the cover up from Thatcher, the Tory government, Murdoch, Mackenzie, News International, South Yorkshire Police, aided and abetted by the West Midlands force, and various other politicians, lawyers, judges, writers et al. Of course, there is a group of people who were part of the mass conspiracy regarding Hillsborough: the Freemasons. This secret society has been 'at it' for many years. The corruptible practices of the Masonic Lodge are well known, no matter how much they try to brush it under their very big carpet. It is a well-known fact that senior and high-ranking police officers were in 'The Black Hand Gang'. Naturally, freemasonry involved people from other walks of life, such as politicians, judges, doctors, journalists, writers etc. Certain links established a mass cover up of monumental proportions.

The 1980s was not a good time, especially in the north of England. There was rampant mass unemployment, riots, deprivation, crime, decaying communities and virtually non-existent public services. The laissez faire ideology of Thatcherism and the obsessive destruction of once proud manufacturing industries, coupled with selling off publicly owned services, and the creation of the 'greed is good' culture, was a diabolical outrage and a heartless invention of a broken and divided society. Then there was her vicious police state.

The long list of industries that went to the wall is a stark reminder of what was lost. There was shipbuilding, steel, car making and, of course, coal. The unions were strong and powerful in those days, they had to be. Gradually, however, Thatcher took away those powers. As union influences crumbled, Thatcher's iron grip on the downtrodden and the poor intensified. Britain was not a democracy anymore, it was a virtual fascist police state and the bullying boys in blue reaped their rewards with vicious intolerance and violent hatred, and were paid handsomely for it. A sickening example of what was wrong with 1980s Britain. To be clear, the right-wing press just devoured and lapped it up. The usual suspects were there: The Daily Mail, The Telegraph, The Daily Express, and, of course, Murdoch's The S*n.

What transpired to a sickening height came in 1984, and the now infamous Miners' Strike. The NUM (National Union of Mineworkers) was the biggest and most powerful union in Britain at that time. Led by the controversial Yorkshireman Arthur Scargill who led the miners head on in a confrontation with Thatcher. It is true that Scargill was a firebrand, some may say a troublemaker or a rebel rouser. I do not hold to that theory. He was a radical left winger, he may even have been a communist, but he was not 'an enemy from within'. That was the predictable and familiar tone voiced by the far right. The smear campaigns orchestrated by Tory HQ were a deliberate policy to wear down the striking miners, and weaken huge public support. The fact that MI5 and the shadowy Department of Dirty Tricks were involved speaks volumes.

Thatcher was hell bent on destroying Arthur Scargill. She would do absolutely anything to achieve her aim, and she would have more than willing participants in the right-wing press. Most notably, Rupert Murdoch and The S*n. Of course, Murdoch had his own union troubles in the form of the Printworkers' Union, and the infamous Wapping incident. Murdoch hated the unions just as much as Thatcher. On a personal note, I got caught up in the Wapping incident. The scenes were chaotic and claustrophobic, to say the least. A stand-off between strikers and the Metropolitan Police. In reality, it was a brutal example of legalised thuggery on the part of the boys in blue, sanctioned by Thatcher and requested by Murdoch. Of course, there are those who claim, quite wrongly, that it was left-wing troublemakers and communist agitators and that 'the police were only doing their job'. This took place in the summer of 1986 amidst violent scenes. Of course, something more horrific, controversial and sickeningly violent and bloody erupted some two years earlier...

Chapter Four

The Battle of Orgreave

There were many pivotal moments during the long running Miners' Strike between 6th March 1984 and 3rd March 1985. A year-long dispute almost to the day. It is true to state that Orgreave is well-known throughout not only the UK, but also the rest of the world. It grabbed global attention. On 18th June 1984, at the British Steel coking plant near Rotherham, a huge stand-off developed between the police and striking miners, who organised a massive picket line and were determined not to allow lorries to pass through. At first, everything was relatively peaceful and good-natured. However, that was not to last. There were a lot of pent-up emotions displayed that day. When your livelihood, your family, and your job are on the line, and you are struggling to make ends meet, naturally you would do almost anything to survive.

On the other side of the coin, you had police officers who were granted huge overtime bonuses, whilst miners starved. Of course, police officers made fun of the fact that they had pot loads of money. They disgracefully mocked and scoffed their prey. Then came the legalised violence and sanctioned thuggery.

Why?

It is perfectly true to state that there was a mass confrontation that day. There was horrific violence from both sides. However, the sickening beatings of miners, skulls cracked, and mob handed bullying were uncalled for, disgustingly vile and beyond any form of reason. Even Arthur Scargill was assaulted by the South Yorkshire bully boys. Of course, police officers were bussed in from a number of forces including West Yorkshire, Lancashire, Nottinghamshire and the West Midlands. However, it was South Yorkshire Police who called the shots. The main man calling those shots was none other than Peter Wright, the recently appointed Chief Constable of South Yorkshire Police. A man who not only had the disgrace of Orgreave on his watch, but some five years later, he was in charge of the biggest sporting disaster in the history of this country: Hillsborough. A total of 97 men, women and children so cruelly lost their lives due to glaring police failures, poor organisation and gross incompetence. Furthermore, Wright was the man who selected David Duckenfield as match commander, and thus caused the deaths of so many innocent people. He oversaw two major incidents of catastrophic proportions. The link between Orgreave and Hillsborough is frighteningly stark. The obvious police mentality of fabrication and falsehood. The same chief constable whose notion was that his officers were not to blame and would be vindicated in any future court proceedings.

The battle lines were drawn, if you forgive the analogy. That day, 18th June 1984, the large field of conflict was the backdrop for a bloody pitched battle, between the police and striking miners. Frankly, the strikers did not stand a chance. The scenes of police on horseback charging the crowd and the violent aggression of the sadistic boys in blue, whose weapon of choice was a truncheon or a baton, was a scene of indiscriminate beatings, with no mercy and zero remorse. The miners, to their credit, gave as good as they got, but they really did not stand a chance. It was only by sheer luck that nobody died that day. And those totally misguided individuals, who preach about arming the police in circumstances such as Orgreave, would have to be prepared for a huge death count and absolute carnage. The way the police behaved that day, and if they were given firearms, the term 'trigger happy' is a nightmare scenario that does not bear thinking about.

Then came the arrests and the subsequent charges and trial. Almost 100 miners were arrested and charged. And what were those charges? These were unlawful assembly, violent disorder and riot.

I hear you saying, 'Riot? What is that?' I do not blame anyone who is confused by such a statement. After all, it iss an archaic law from the Middle Ages. It is not used in more modern times. It was prevalent in the early 19th century and the horrific killing of innocent people at the Peterloo Massacre of 1819 at Saint Peter's Field in Manchester. The last time it was used was in the early years of the 20th century, in Birkenhead. This ancient law carried a sentence of life imprisonment.

So, why was the charge of riot implemented in modern Britain?

This old law states that 'riot has a term of life imprisonment'. The absolute arrogance of the authorities in this matter was to state that 'we will make an example of those thugs and what they did'. It is a great pity that nothing was done to the *real* thugs, namely Thatcher's right-wing militia. Would you expect anything else? The veil of corruption, cover up and fabrication. A shockingly, predictable story.

However, there are some very stupid people within the framework of law and order. The very short-sighted decision to go all out for a conviction of riot was a very fatal mistake. A mistake that would be costly. The trial itself was full of contradictions, even the most right-wing of judges would struggle to agree with the police, and indeed, Thatcher herself.

The indisputable fact that thirty-nine miners were not only found not guilty, but charges against them were thrown out in court. The official court verdict, written down in law stated 'acquitted', and the evidence that South Yorkshire Police submitted was 'unreliable'. Echoes of Hillsborough immediately spring to mind. The trial itself was a major victory for the miners. Yet, some six months or so later, the most bitter and controversial industrial dispute was called off. Why? The fact that the vicious far right government under the hated Thatcher, held all the cards. The abuse of power manifested itself through the media and the police. The 'enemy from within' propaganda tool was more akin to Josef Goebbels, Hitler and the Nazis. The vicious bullying of mining communities by stopping strike pay and starving families to submission was immoral, vile, heartless and without compassion. It was only through the miners' wives, who bravely set up soup kitchens, organised handouts and fundraising to support the miners, that they managed to exist and survive.

Then came the scabs from the Nottinghamshire coal fields, and the cowardly traitor, Roy Lynk. If Thatcher ever ran a Punch and Judy show, Lynk would have been the main puppet. Then there was the seizure of NUM funds and the MI5's dirty tricks campaign, where they labelled Arthur Scargill as a communist agitator. Whether he was a communist or not is clearly irrelevant. This country supposedly upholds the values of fairness and freedom of speech. In the horrific and uncompromising times of Thatcher's Britain, we suffered more than a decade of poverty, decay, isolation, greed, a broken society and deprivation, just so the corporate fat cats and the yuppie greed merchants could get their good life, and sod the rest.

At the end of the day, the Miners' Strike of 1984/85 was doomed to fail. Not because of the miners themselves, nor their families or people who supported them, but the gross display of a virtual police state, and an unfair society, coupled with the right-wing media domination in this country. Whilst Thatcher arrogantly pursued her hatred of the left, and the insistence that Scargill was 'public enemy number one', what about those she held up as so called 'politicians and leaders of virtue'?

We all know about her 'romantic love-in' with Reagan, whilst Denis guzzled on the gin. What about Pinochet, the far right dictator from Chile? A monster who ordered the brutal slaying of fellow Chileans on a mass scale. This despot always had a dislike for its near neighbour, Argentina. So, when another despot, namely Thatcher, needed some help, a hand of friendship was offered. So, her illegal war in the Falklands was set to go. So why did we go to war in the Falklands? Was it down to Argentine sabre-rattling? There had been no animosity regarding the claim to the islands apart from a few diplomatic murmurings, here and there. It is true to state that the old Peronist system had had its day, and a military junta was an inevitable conclusion. So, when General Galtieri took over in Argentina, something was bound to happen that would cause instability and conflict. It was like music to Thatcher's ears. She was an opportunist. The country was in turmoil, through mass unemployment, division, abject poverty and rising crime. She and her policies were deeply unpopular. The next general election was pivotal. The notion that a 'convenient war' was not lost on her. The jingoistic, rallying cry would save her and the government. The fact of national pride would go down well in certain areas of the country.

So, there you have it, a well thought out policy to seize back the Falklands no matter what the cost. The real reason why Thatcher went to war over the Falklands was purely a selfish one. In public, it was all about protecting British citizens and the right to defend a British territory. The notion being that Argentina broke international law, and the United Kingdom had the right to defend itself.

In private, however, it was much more controversial and shocking. Many lives were lost, on both sides, just so that Thatcher could maintain power. It was an opportunity that she could not afford to miss. The war boosted her ratings back home in opinion polls. The war was the one indisputable fact that won Thatcher the general election of 1983. The crisis in Britain was forgotten, and national pride was the fundamentally most important factor.

Moreover, a year or so after the election, Thatcher went to war again. This time it was the miners, the NUM and Arthur Scargill: the enemy from within.

Chapter Five

Justice Delayed is Justice Denied

After the biggest sporting disaster in British history, the complexities of the legal framework came into play. From day one, it was perfectly clear what was both conspired and transpired. From the day itself, 15th April 1989, a cover up ensued, starting with Duckenfield's disgraceful lie. A vile smell of cowardice and falsehood. On the journey home, having been emotionally ripped apart and rocked to the core, the 'broken gate' scenario came into play. When Duckenfield met up with Graham Kelly, the secretary of the FA, the discussion was around crowd trouble, disorder, drink, and fans without tickets. All false allegations and lies. The world knows that now. Of course, Kelly had much to lose and everything to gain by running with that false narrative. The ground was unsafe, but Kelly insisted it was not. He chose the venue, it was his call. The Green Guide, which focused on safety at football grounds, warned of foreseeable problems at Hillsborough. So, why was the 1989 semi-final played at Hillsborough? Why were the 'near misses' at Hillsborough in previous years not investigated? What role did the structural engineers, Eastwoods, play in the safety procedures?

The key question that needs addressing is who really held the key as regards to the semi-final. There were a few interested parties, such as the Football Association, Sheffield Wednesday, Eastwoods, Sheffield City Council, and, of course, South Yorkshire Police. The fact is, in semi-finals played in 1981, 1987 and 1988, there were significant injuries to spectators at those games. Yet, between 1981 and 1987, semi-finals were not played there. That begs the question, why? If you speak to fans of Tottenham Hotspur, Wolverhampton Wanderers, Coventry City, Leeds United, Liverpool and Nottingham Forest, you will find the answer. Hillsborough was a ground that was chronically unsafe. There were fundamental problems. The most serious problem was at the Leppings Lane end. A tight bottleneck on the street behind the ground. The limited space was a virtual death trap, especially at big matches like FA Cup semi-finals. Furthermore, when you have inadequate policing strategies, weak leadership and gross incompetence, then you have a mass tragedy on your hands. If you have an unsuitable stadium, safety features not implemented, turnstiles woefully inadequate, then you are heading for a terrible situation to develop. At Hillsborough in 1989, it was a combination of poor policing, missed opportunities, in relation to Duckenfield failing to delay the kick off, not adhering to the filtering system used at previous semi-finals, and the absolute incompetence of not closing off the tunnel, that Lord Justice Taylor stated in his interim report was 'a blunder of the first magnitude'.

Even Taylor mentioned the lies told by senior officers of South Yorkshire Police, but praised the rank-and-file junior officers of the force. Moreover, Taylor stated that 'alcohol was not a significant feature in relation to the disaster'.

If SYP were going to get an easy ride, then they were sadly mistaken. They were expecting to be let off the hook. The Taylor Report had some good and very valid points around Hillsborough. Sadly, though, there were some glaring contradictions. When Taylor openly criticised eminent doctors for appearing on national television, he poured scorn over the issue, claiming it was 'unhelpful'. When you have eminent and well thought of clinicians, like Professor John Ashton who was at that game, then you hope that someone with such expertise would be called upon to offer advice and not be ostracised publicly for appearing on television. You only have to look at Professor Ashton's achievements and expert analysis to realise that this man speaks the truth, and with common sense. To have a glowing reputation ruined by Taylor was an absolute outrage. What Professor Ashton did was what we all did who were at Hillsborough, he spoke the truth. The real truth. To criticise the ambulance service (SYMAS) is not some falsehood or a deliberate character assassination, it is fact. Professor Ashton tried valiantly to save lives. How is that unhelpful? His description of the carnage on that pitch was an interesting one, in which he said, 'It was comparable to something like the Somme.'

The cover up had begun in earnest, from the blatant Duckenfield lie, and would shockingly go on unabated for over a quarter of a century. It is very true to state that justice delayed is justice denied.

Chapter Six

Miscarriages of Justice

To wait so long for some feeling of rightful justice is something which is immensely frustrating, deeply traumatic and the term, 'banging your head against a brick wall' is a very apt sentiment to make. For the bereaved families and survivors of Hillsborough, that is what it was like, year after year, decade after decade. The same model was applied in the shifting sands of cover up, corruption and collusion. It has to be noted that there were more than 97 deaths in regards to Hillsborough. Over these long years, a lot of people have passed on, whether through failing health, old age, and even suicide.

What you can state unequivocally is that those in authority, whether they were politicians, the judiciary, police or other emergency services, and the misjudgement of those interested parties in relation to the campaigners was a catastrophic error on their part. They thought and expected that we would go away and give up. Not a chance. The familiar statement has never been more relevant: you picked on the wrong city.

So, what were those miscarriages of justice?

In those long, dark days of the past, when victory seemed a long and very distant horizon, and that nothing was possible, where we had to defend those who died, to defend ourselves as survivors, to defend the bereaved families, you can state clearly that in darkness you can see even the slightest of a flickering light. We had to focus on that.

When the Taylor Report was published in January 1990, less than a year after the tragedy, initial optimism soon diminished. Whilst there were some valid points raised around blatant lies of drink and ticketlessness, as well as lack of care and control and the role of Duckenfield, it still had some very fatal flaws. Furthermore, South Yorkshire Police were confident that their 'version' of events would come out in the inquests. They were already planning their hideous attack on the survivors and bereaved families. And the so-called 'impartial' role of the coroner, Stefan Popper, would come into play. He was already involved in certain procedures from day one. The shameful blood alcohol tests on the dead, including young children, was insisted by Popper, as was the awful identification process in the club gymnasium. It kind of sticks in the throat how the British legal system works, or I should say, does not work. So, there you have a coroner in charge of proceedings. A coroner who used a false narrative and dubious interpretation. Who ordered blood alcohol tests on all who died, including, shockingly, young children. The way the bereaved families and survivors were treated was absolutely rotten and shocking to the core. There were many dubious decisions made in that court in Sheffield.

The inquests began on 19th November 1990. South Yorkshire Police were adamant that the tragedy occurred due to drunken, ticketless fans who arrived late. This is despite what the Taylor Report had said in their findings. The fact is in August 1990, the Director of Public Prosecutions decided there was 'insufficient evidence' to press charges over Hillsborough. The tone and language had been firmly set.

A coroner's court is meant to find out what happened to loved ones. It is supposed to be impartial. It is not a criminal court, although there is a jury present. There should be no accusations as such, and nobody is on trial. Yet, the first Hillsborough inquests were nothing more than a trial with vicious accusations, smears, lies and falsehood. It was not an inquest, it was more akin to a kangaroo court. It was, without doubt, an organised and callous fit up. You need to look beyond the surface and the deep-rooted cover up. You need to ask questions. Why?

Why? Why was the 3:15 cut-off point insisted upon by Popper?

After all, there were some victims still alive beyond that time. The most familiar one was Kevin Williams, who survived beyond 4 p.m. Well, young Kevin's profile did not fit the false narrative. It did not fit with the cover up. Debra Martin was a special constable on duty that day at Hillsborough. She also had nursing and dental experience, and she tended to Kevin that afternoon. Debra Martin stated that Kevin uttered the word 'Mum' shortly before he died. Of course, Debra Martin was pressured and lent on to change her story.

Why? Why were West Midlands Police brought in to investigate Hillsborough?

You really could not make it up, could you? To select a force so deep-rooted in corruption and sanctioned criminality beggars belief. There is a catalogue of wrongdoing, ranging from overtime fiddling, late night drinking, police brutality, forced confessions and extreme interrogations. It is well known that the Serious Crime Squad of West Midlands Police used a technique called 'plastic bagging' to interrogate victims, and demanded forced confessions with relish, intimidation and vicious threats. This type of police thuggery was used against the Birmingham Six in the 1970s.

The man in charge of the West Midlands Serious Crime Squad was none other than Chief Superintendent Stanley Beechey. The word 'corrupt' does not fully describe him. The man was a disgrace, and would do anything to stay on top through bribery, threats and fabrication. However, the net was closing in on Beechey. Even the Chief Constable, Sir Geoffrey Dear, who cannot readily be described as being whiter than white, was deeply concerned. He decided to disband the Serious Crime Squad. This could have serious implications on the force. There were investigations but, surprise, surprise, nothing came of it. The standard response of 'insufficient evidence' was given. And what of Beechey? A slap on the wrist? Suspension? A cosy little chat down at the Masonic Lodge?

No.

Unbelievably, disgracefully, Beechey was offered the role at the inquests as a Coroner's Officer. So, there you have a corrupt high-ranking police detective, an equally corrupt force, another equally corrupt force and a corrupt coroner. It does not take a genius to work out what transpired next. There was a procedure to allow 'selected witnesses' to appear before the inquests. Those who had strong evidence against the police and other interested parties were deliberately not called. Whereas local residents and selected publicans who voiced their opinions around drink, ticketlessness, bad behaviour and the like, were warmly welcomed to give their 'evidence'. How can a young lad urinating in a garden on Leppings Lane be deemed responsible for what happened that day?

The inquests were a travesty. A purposeful attempt to smear the families and survivors, any way possible, no holds barred. There was a complex web of deceit. A complicated maze of corruption and collusion. The list was seemingly endless, and a vast mechanism of individuals and organisations. There were survivors and witnesses who were aggressively challenged with unrepentant questioning along the lines of 'we don't believe you' or 'we don't think you were really there'. Then it became politicised. 'Are you a socialist agitator?' Or 'are you a member of the communist party?'

They, being West Midlands Police officers, would try anything to pressure those who they deemed as unreliable or potential troublemakers. There was a lot at stake and a lot to lose. Their intention was to produce an orchestrated and elaborate cover up, with absolutely no respect or thought for the bereaved families or survivors. It was all about creating a false narrative and protecting self-interests as well as fat pensions.

The inquests lasted longer than anticipated. The disgraceful condemnation of those who died, through the analysis of the level of blood alcohol in the system as noted in the mini inquests, was a thoughtless, discriminatory and degrading part of the proceedings. Yet again, it was the police response to focus on drink, and it was supported and backed up by Popper who, as already stated, ordered and sanctioned such tests to be carried out on the night of 15th April 1989. A position in which he stated he was 'perfectly happy with'.

To be one of the families, or a survivor, having to sit through months of agonising horror, condemnation and lies, is without question, an unbearable scenario. Such resolve and commitment makes you a special person, with a strong iron will and absolute strength in impossible adversity. I totally commend them for that. No doubt they are a true inspiration.

The verdicts, which were announced in September 1991, came with no surprise to many. Naturally, the families and survivors still hoped for a positive outcome. However, it was the same verdict for each and every one of the victims: accidental death.

There was a mixture of outrage, disbelief, anger and many, many tears. The only fitting response was a rendition of 'You'll Never Walk Alone'.

There were many who simply would not give up, no matter how insurmountable the odds. There would be a lot of time to wait. A time to take stock. But this was not over. Not by a long chalk.

During the early to mid-90s, there was a sea change in British politics. It was a gradual one. The Labour party was unelectable under Michael Foot. Sad to say, but perfectly true. As a lifelong Labour voter and supporter, that pains me to say it. There was a civil war within the Labour party, and the obsession with knocking down the Militant Tendency was a situation that was both regrettable and unfortunate, and only helped the Tories. It was a no-win situation. Neil Kinnock, when he was elected Labour leader, waged a war against Liverpool's militants and especially deputy council leader, Derek Hatton. The deep mistrust from both sides of the Labour party, only served as a detrimental effect. Kinnock lost the general election, with a lot of media exposure from the far-right newspaper barons, most notably Murdoch and The S*n.

It had been almost twenty years since Labour had been in power. After Kinnock resigned, the search was on to find a new Labour leader. In 1992, John Smith QC was elected to the post. A very eloquent lawyer, who was the MP for Monkton East, and was the one Labour politician whom the Tories genuinely feared. A robust public speaker and brilliant orator, John Smith was the obvious choice. Sadly, within two years, he was dead. He had a fatal heart attack in London, and was laid to rest on the idyllic island of Iona. The best prime minister we never had. So, where would we go from here?

The coronation of Tony Blair was very much on the cards. I, like many others, was hoodwinked, conned, by Blair. It was something fresh, new and vibrant. You could ignore the toothpaste grin, even the smugness. The Tories were drinking in the last chance saloon, and the self-styled 'New Labour' under Blair were heading for a huge landslide and a remarkable victory. Remember the old saying, 'be careful what you wish for, you might just get it'? After a wave of euphoria and self-congratulation, it was time to 'repair the country'. Whilst in opposition, the Labour party confirmed its commitment to give some kind of justice over Hillsborough. Well, it is perfectly true to state that governments change but the lies remain the same.

In 1997, following the election victory, Blair announced his cabinet. His new Home Secretary was to be Jack Straw, the then MP for Blackburn. So, Jack, the Man of Straw, took up his position in the Home Office…

The second miscarriage of justice was about to be implemented. True to his word, Straw was about to 'help' the Hillsborough families and survivors out. He appointed Lord Justice Stuart-Smith to oversee a judicial scrutiny into Hillsborough. It was going to be 'thorough' and 'without limitations'.

A group of family members met 'Murray in a Hurry' on the Liverpool waterfront. Murray was his first name. Shockingly, he mocked some members of the group, as they had problems getting there on time. His ghastly comment was along the lines of, 'Are you like Liverpool supporters? Always running late?' That crass statement caused a furore. He was linking Hillsborough with late arrivals. There was deep anger that day, with some refusing to meet with him. He duly apologised, but the damage was done and the tone set.

The judicial scrutiny was another travesty and undoubtedly another miscarriage of justice. Stuart-Smith would only accept evidence that was totally new in regards to Hillsborough. The limitations placed on the review was unhelpful to say the least. Despite the obvious assertion that evidence taken after 3:15 p.m. was not permitted in the original inquests, Stuart-Smith refused to allow this as new evidence. Why? After all, it was not allowed by Popper so it was *new* evidence. Another example of the deliberate and orchestrated cover up over Hillsborough. Another example of the corrupt legal system looking after their own. The whole sorry story of cover up and denial was plain to see.

When the opposition achieves power and becomes the new government, all of a sudden, things change. This happened in 1997 with New Labour. In opposition, Jack Straw, as Shadow Home Secretary, wanted to 're-write the wrongs over Hillsborough'. Sure enough, within six weeks of coming into office, a judicial scrutiny was ordered. Hope was raised amongst the families and survivors. The scrutiny would be held at the Maritime Museum in Liverpool, over several days. Another positive. Sadly, that was about as good as it got. Jack, the Man of Straw, saw to that. He had already decided the fate of the scrutiny within a few short days. The hypocritical nature was there. He then wrote to his mate, Blair: nothing can be done, or should be done, over Hillsborough. Of course, Blair had already stated that Hillsborough would not be reopened. His assertion being, 'What is the point?'

In reality, Murdoch was his paymaster who had turned his back on the Tories, and instead supported New Labour. It was all about power and the abuse of it. Blair did not want to offend Murdoch, so Hillsborough would remain 'silent'. Home secretary after home secretary toed the line.

It would take a very special politician to break the chains of injustice.

So, what about Straw? It is worth noting and pointing out that he had 'regrets' over Hillsborough. He stated that 'I wish I could turn back the clock'. Well, Jack, so could we, to before 15th April 1989. The damage had been done and it was on your watch. You should have focused on the mass cover up of the biggest sporting disaster in the history of this country. But, of course, you had other pressing issues, like getting your own son off on a drugs charge, for selling and smoking dope. There would be another three years before court proceedings involving Hillsborough would come back to the public's attention.

A new millennium. A new century. Yet, there still had not been any justice for the 96. In 2000, a private prosecution was taken out by members of the HFSG (Hillsborough Family Support Group). The prospect of getting Duckenfield in the dock was not lost on anyone who was there.

So, a balmy June came, and the venue was Leeds Crown Court. Those lovely policemen were filming everything around them, making sure that Bettison's Bullies got the 'right images'. In reality, they were 'keeping their eye on any potential troublemakers'. It really does beggar belief that the families and survivors, who were at that court, would even remotely think about 'kicking off'. They were there to try to get some kind of justice for their loved ones over Hillsborough. That would be the last thing on their minds, their sole focus was the private prosecution of Duckenfield and Murray, the two most senior officers on duty that day: 15th April 1989.

Then we got people who felt it was in their best interest to call for a halt to the case as it was 'unfair'. Unfair? It was *unfair* that 97 innocent men, women and children were mercilessly crushed to death. It was *unfair* that survivors were rounded upon and falsely accused of being 'drunk' or 'ticketless', and were blatantly lied about and smeared regarding 'robbing the dead' or 'urinating on corpses'. It was *unfair* to use vile smears, outlandish fabrications and an orchestrated cover up to get the ones responsible for the tragedy off the hook. It was *unfair* for survivors, who should have been treated as heroes as they ferried the injured and rescued the dying, to be falsely labelled as 'hooligans'.

So, who made this statement?

Shockingly, it came from the vicar or minister from a local church or chapel. A number of posters and leaflets were found at the locality. Naturally, they soon 'disappeared' when this so-called 'Christian' was found out. Absolutely disgusting.

What about the private prosecution itself? Some say it was a 'show trial'. The legal parameters set were 'not helpful'. The specific limitations were 'more restricted' in relation to the time frame, even the 'cut off point' of 3:15 was changed to an even more restrictive 3:06; the time the game was stopped. The team of lawyers and solicitors, whilst they did their best, were not up to scratch. I know that seems brutal, but it is the fact.

When such a monumental tragedy occurs, you are always going to get disagreements, differing opinions and even arguments. It is quite natural. These days, I do not take sides in this issue. I have learnt and grown. What is in the past stays in the past. The whole HFSG vs. HJC thing was very counterproductive. It only helped the detractors and those who criticised us. Personally, I am glad to be out of it. Life is too short, and there is no reason for regrets.

So, back to the case at Leeds Crown Court. There was no sense, almost from the outset, that it would deliver justice. The language from the judge, Lord Justice Hooper, spoke the same corrupt indignation. He felt pity for the defendants and insisted that if convicted, it would be 'unsafe' to send them to prison. So, here was a judge who voiced his own opinions, when he should have been wholly impartial. Here was a judge who stated that there would be no prison term, despite the fact the trial had not even started. Hooper claimed lives could be in danger if he jailed the defendants. A trial that was corrupted with bias and lack of fairness. It was a case of families vs. the system.

At the end of the trial, the inevitable conclusion was reached. Murray got off. Duckenfield was not convicted. The one bright, positive outcome was that whilst he was not convicted, he was not cleared either, as the jury could not agree on a verdict.

A few years on, Murray died. Hooper retired with his obligatory knighthood for 'good service'. The bereaved families were further away from justice than ever before.

Chapter Seven

Hergest: A Personal Tragedy

When you lose a member of your family, it really hits you hard, of sledgehammer proportions. As regards to Hillsborough, although I was never related to those beautiful 97 angels, I felt I knew them, as if they were my brothers and sisters. I was there, in a physical sense, when they left us. I was there in Leppings Lane, in those central pens, in the steep, dark tunnel and the 6:1 gradient. There was a deep sense of loss. Naturally, the pain that the families suffered is totally beyond comparison. After all, you do not expect a loved one to go to a football match and never return home. Neither do you expect to be treated with contempt by the system. You also do not expect your loved ones to be savagely accused of 'killing their own'. Furthermore, you do not expect, as bereaved families in deep, traumatic shock, to be interrogated in the identification process in such a callous way, with wild accusations about tickets, the amount of drink consumed, and time of arrival. To top it all off, you had the sickening denial of basic human rights, the abuse of power and the heartless demand of not being able to touch the body of your special loved ones.

There is no logic to it all. There is no level of the depravity of evil that was imposed. How so many of the wonderful families kept their cool, restraint and peaceful integrity is beyond me. There should have been violent rage, screaming discontent and intense physical assault. But there was not. That is what makes the Hillsborough families so very special. God bless you all.

I would like to take you to 24th November 1994. It was over five and a half years after Hillsborough. My struggles with PTSD were at its height. My darkest days. I survived on vast amounts of alcohol and violent rage. Not a very nice combination. The chronic symptoms were plain to see. The hellish nightmares, the awful panic attacks, very vivid flashbacks, deep-seated paranoia, shocking survivor guilt, frustration, rage, low self-esteem, absolutely zero confidence and the screaming, crying and waking up in cold sweats. That is what it was like, living with PTSD.

My brother, Anthony, was three years younger than me. Anyone who has a brother, or indeed a sister, will know what it is like with a younger sibling. We fought like cats and dogs. Summer holidays were, well, interesting to say the least. Yet, when we got in trouble, we were there for each other. Anthony had suffered from severe depression and deep anxiety ever since his teenage years. He had to be sectioned twice under the Mental Health Act, and had tried to take his own life. After the attempted suicide incident, he was hauled into the police station. There was no sympathy or thought for his mental state, it was all about cautioning or charging him. Is it little wonder that I have no time for the police, given how my experiences have hit me square in the face? In the end, Anthony faced a stark choice: be charged or be sectioned.

Anthony was placed on a mental health ward. It was horrible, and that is being kind. It had a bad reputation. Basically, the patients were left to their own devices and were drugged up like zombies. Truly awful. We, as a family, were not accepting this crass treatment. So, we went to see our GP. After much arm twisting and repeated conversations, the doctor relented and arranged for an appointment at another hospital, around a thirty-minute drive away. This was a totally different scenario. The mental health unit, masked inside a large hospital, was absolutely fantastic. The psychiatrist insisted that the residents—he deplored the term patients—had to exercise both the mind as well as the body. They had to take part in routine tasks, such as making their own beds, washing up, cleaning etc. There was to be a strong exercise regime, and that they were expected to attend various courses and classes to stimulate the mind. It was all very positive and, at that time, ground breaking.

Within a few months, Anthony was a totally different person. It was almost as if he had been transformed. He gained bucket loads of confidence, and his low self-esteem evaporated. We were all pleased by this amazing progress. In the summer of 1994, Anthony applied to go to university. A sure sign he had developed psychologically. He successfully obtained a place at Bangor University, in Gwynedd, North Wales. Anthony had decided to study Forestry. He was always an outdoor type; he absolutely loved sea fishing as a prime example. So, he was set for university life.

Anthony started his degree in September 1994. He was happy enough at the beginning of his time at Bangor. It wasn't until November that we thought something was wrong. Anthony kept ringing home, several times a day. He wanted to come home. It was decided that my dad and myself would drive to Chester and meet him at the railway station. In what seemed like an eternity, we waited, waited and waited. Anthony did not show. We had to make a decision and decided we should drive to Bangor, along the A55.

After arriving in Bangor, we had to find the university, then the halls of residence. The next step was to find his room and request access. Once we got into the room, we were shocked to find what a state the room was in. I noticed a piece of scrap paper on his desk. There was a scribbled message written on it. I could tell it was Anthony's writing. The message read:

THE DEVIL IS GOING TO KILL ME.
GOD IS COMING.

All the classic signs of a severe psychotic episode.

After calling home, my mum told us that North Wales Police had contacted her, explaining that Anthony had been picked up and taken to Prestatyn Police Station. So off we went again, along the A55, this time in the other direction. When we arrived in Prestatyn, we needed to locate the police station, which we did within a few minutes. We found out that Anthony had been picked up in a deeply distressed state, amongst the sand dunes on the beach. He was wearing only one sock. The police doctor examined him and insisted that he needed to be transferred to a mental health unit… you guessed it, in Bangor. So, off we went once more, on our North Wales rally.

It seemed to take an age to find the hospital. Eventually, we were successful. The hospital in Bangor was a huge building. The Hergest Unit was a 'secure' psychiatric facility inside the hospital grounds. By this time, both my dad and myself were totally shattered, physically, emotionally and psychologically. I really could not take any more stress. My mental state was fragile, to say the least. We approached the unit, and waited until we were let in. We sat and waited a little longer. Eventually, we were greeted by the psychiatrist, a youngish man, who I would say to be in his mid-thirties. He explained about Anthony's condition and state of mind. We were told that he could not be released from the unit. There had to be further investigations and tests carried out. I will never, ever forget his name: Doctor Thomas Mcmonagle. We were then allowed to meet with Anthony. He seemed very quiet, withdrawn and sombre. Maybe that was the medication he was on. We greeted each other and hugged. I will always remember those few words that he spoke: 'I have changed.'

That was it. All very short and not particularly sweet. It was the last time we spoke. The last time we saw him alive. My mum never had that chance. That deeply upsets me even now. I did at least come back from Hillsborough, alive. Anthony, sadly, did not make it. He did not survive. It was in a totally different context. It was just one person in turmoil. One family in grief. It was not spread across the newspapers or splashed on the TV news. Apart from a few local articles in the regional press, there was nothing. At least we were thankful for that.

Everything went quiet for a few minutes. Somewhat eerily quiet. However, all of a sudden, there was this terrific bang. We did not know what it was all about. The staff drank tea; they did not seem bothered. Then Mcmonagle hurriedly arrived at the scene. He told us that Anthony had managed to get out through a window, and onto a slate roof. We really could not take it in. How the hell could he escape from a secure unit? Why were the staff sipping tea and gossiping? Why did they not help in the search? There were questions that needed addressing. This hellish day had knocked us sideways. We stayed a very uncomfortable night in one of the family rooms. Honestly, we could not get a wink of sleep. It was impossible.

The following morning, we decided to drive back home to Lancashire. Before we left, Mcmonagle actually criticised us for not taking part in the search, and asked us if we really cared. The fact that it was dark, cold, and we were devoid of any energy, did not register with him. Furthermore, we did not know the area, where were we supposed to go? That was the most crass statement a health professional could possibly make. My brother freed himself from a supposed secure mental health unit, not knowing his own mind, and scared and frightened to his wits end, to the point it led to his horrific death. So, who was responsible for Anthony's death. Doctor Mcmonagle?

The drive home was hideous and unbearable. We never spoke a word, and the grief and hurt pained our faces. A well of tears filled my dad's eyes. I knew Anthony was dead. I had that gut feeling, and a shocking fear of dread. I just knew. I hated this life. These two horrendous tragedies, some five years apart, were soul destroying, unbearable and deeply disturbing. Looking back, I wondered how I managed to cope. In fact, I don't think I really did. I am very conscious of the fact, and very much questioning myself in the process.

Why the hell did I not take my own life?

When we finally got back home, everything seemed so unreal. We just had to wait for news, good or bad. My dad went straight to bed, to try to get some sleep. My mum went to the local shop, just around the corner. I was alone for a brief few minutes. It only takes a few minutes. A police car pulled up. At that moment, I knew. Anthony, my younger brother, was dead. You cannot prepare for such moments as that. It floors you, rips you to shreds, beats you senseless. It knocks the stuffing out of you. The worst thing was seeing my mum's shocked, tearful face, as she hurriedly came down the driveway. A young police constable was at the door. I invited him in.

My mum asked him, 'Have you found Anthony?'

The policeman was probably inexperienced, and more than likely had never had to give the news of a loved one's death. 'We have, yes, in a way.'

In a way? I ran up the stairs to wake up my dad. When we came down, the constable continued. 'It appears that he has taken his own life.'

Why would he make that statement? Given the time frame, he was unsure what the cause of death was. He certainly should not be guessing the outcome of Anthony's death. There would not have been the time to arrange a post mortem to try to establish the cause. A young, inexperienced PC maybe, but surely common sense would have told him not to voice his own opinions.

We were rocked, shaken to the core, totally not taking it all in. My mum and dad were uncontrollable. We all hugged. I am not much of a 'touchy feely' kind of person. I usually keep things more or less private, and do not show much emotion. I tend to bottle things up, until a volcanic eruption occurs inside my head. Then, I hit the 'rage' button and let it all rip. My parents told me I was their 'rock'. I didn't feel like it.

When Anthony died, there eventually had to be an inquest to establish a cause of death. That was a few months down the line. His death was horrific. A cold, dark November night. He was in a hell of a state, he clearly did not know where he was or what he was doing. There is a village that runs alongside the very busy A55 dual carriageway, called Llandygai. From the bridge above, you can see a concrete footpath that cyclists use. It is at least a fifty-foot drop from the bridge to the path. Anyone who fell from that bridge would not stand a chance. Any death would not only be horrific, but the suffering of head trauma, internal bleeding and the ghastly scene of a skull unrecognisable does not bear thinking about. The young cyclist who found Anthony must have suffered deep psychological trauma. I am sorry for what he or she had to endure. I was thankful that I did not have to identify the body. My mental turmoil just could not take it. After all, I had seen so much death to last a lifetime, indeed many lifetimes.

The time had come to arrange the funeral. We were brought up as Roman Catholics, although both Anthony and myself had lapsed from the faith. Yet, I had this sudden urge to go back to church. Something was within me to rekindle my faith. I needed that strength. When the parish priest came to see us at home, not only was he so wonderfully caring and compassionate, he understood our immense pain. When I explained my situation regarding non-attendance at church—I had not attended mass for some seventeen years—Father Leo did not judge me. He simply stated, 'general absolution', which basically means that sins in the past had been forgiven, and that I was free to attend mass and could take Holy Communion. That was a real relief for me. To this very day, I have been attending church for more than twenty-five years.

When it came to the funeral, which was a Requiem Mass, which I recall as being on a Friday, my stomach rattled and I felt physically sick. There were a lot of people there to pay their respects. I know it sounds brutally harsh, but I did not want anyone there. I wanted them all to simply go away. The fear of the day was overwhelming me to the point of wishing that I could be swallowed whole. As PTSD days go, this was probably the worst, apart from Hillsborough itself.

It was all very overbearing as we gathered at church. As I sat in the funeral limousine, the fear, the looks and the staring really got to me. Yes, it was deep paranoia, but all that my mind could tell me was that they hated me, they glared at me, they were suspicious of me. I even had a thought that flashed across my mind, that told me they thought I was to blame for Anthony's death. In reality, that was not the case, but this freak show that was my life with PTSD, would not let it go. The processional circus as we walked up towards the altar was overwhelming, to say the least. Was it a circus, or were we like wild animals being looked at and examined?

The service itself was very moving. The church was full. I cannot thank Anthony's friends enough. They all came to pay their respects: Simon, Leonard, Paul, Phil, Sutt. They can be forgiven for the over the top floral tribute in the shape of a large cross with 'TONE' emblazoned on it! It was just a very long and emotional day. After the Requiem, we had to slowly journey up to the crematorium for the next part of the proceedings. The cremation was not as long, less than half an hour. Then it was back home for the wake. I really was struggling at this point. The mourners scoffed sarnies and the like from the buffet, and devoured what alcohol there was. It really did stick in the throat. The Bangor lecturers and students were sat there for what seemed like forever. I just really wanted them to leave. I know that might seem terrible or heartless, but it was just how I was feeling at that point. We never heard from them again. I just had to get out of the house. I was attending a training course in nearby Nelson. I took my young nephew, David, with me. I just had to be somewhere else.

As the months rolled on, we had to steel ourselves for the forthcoming inquest, which was scheduled for early March 1995. However, I was spent. Emotionally, physically and psychologically. There was no stomach for a fight. You may see that as a weakness, but that 'weakness' had a hell of a lot of baggage. I just could not cope with the inquest. My dad went with a solicitor for legal support. Looking back, I really should have been with him. That was a very deep regret on my part. I have looked through all the legal papers regarding Anthony. His medical history, the many issues with mental health, and the ultimate struggle with paranoid schizophrenia that cost him his life. I have also looked at the role of the Hergest Unit and Mcmonagle. It is perfectly true that the medical profession have orchestrated cover ups, just like politicians and the police. They lie. They fabricate. They collude. They smear. The papers referenced details of the night Anthony got out of the Hergest Unit. Of course, they changed the narrative. The claims of Anthony 'discharging himself' were a total, absolute lie. The indisputable fact was that Anthony got out through a window and onto a slate roof that contributed to his death. Another fact was that this was a supposedly 'secure unit'. Anthony was in their care, and it was their duty to protect him and keep him safe, especially due to the fact that Anthony was in a very fragile and severe mental state. Furthermore, to disgracefully blame us, as family, for not doing anything in relation to the search, is wholly inappropriate and shifting the blame.

The inquest had three possible verdicts. These were suicide, misadventure or open verdict. Obviously, we hoped for the latter. Even though Anthony was very seriously ill with severe psychological problems and suffered from paranoid schizophrenia, we still maintained that he did not take his own life. The coroner actually agreed with this. His statement was pretty clear. The way Anthony fell and the position of the body lent itself to a tragic accident and not taking his own life. However, the coroner could not give a verdict of misadventure but he also could not give a verdict of suicide. The most logical outcome had to be one of an open verdict. He reiterated his assertion that he had to be a hundred percent sure to go with the other two options and that the open verdict was the only course of action that could be possibly taken.

Yet the same old cover up reared its ugly head once more. There was no mention of the Hergest Unit and its failings to protect a vulnerable person, and a dereliction of duty of care. There was no mention of how someone in a severe mental state could easily break out of a secure unit and that staff were very lax in responding. There was no mention of the disgraceful slur against the family for not joining in with the search. *Nothing*.

We, as a family, were left deeply disappointed and wanted to pursue things further. Yet, as always seems to be the case, the poor do not get justice. We were denied legal aid, so that put a stop to any chance of justice for Anthony.

What is even more galling, and a real kick in the teeth, is the fact that Mcmonagle slipped off back to Ireland, and has been a so-called 'high flier' in psychiatrist terms in Dublin. Disgraceful beyond reason.

As a footnote to this chapter, I would just like to say that this is not the end. This has not finished, even a quarter of a century on. I am determined to carry on this fight. When all of this transpired in 1994/95, I really was not there for Anthony. I know my parents said that I was their 'rock' but that was just them being kind. I certainly didn't feel like a rock. My head wasn't right, nor was my desire to fight for Anthony and his memory. As I have already stated, I had no stomach for a fight. I was finished.

However, I did not have to search very far for unbreakable inspiration. The Hillsborough families and survivors supplied that in bucket loads. For over a quarter of a century, they fought despite the setbacks, despite insurmountable odds, despite all the disgraceful smears and lies, and the now very familiar false narratives. They did not give up. They would not go away. They persevered. They won.

Now is the time for Anthony's voice to be heard, through me.

Chapter Eight

The Road is Long

The twentieth anniversary of the Hillsborough disaster was one of those pivotal, defining, landmark moments that we all remember. There was no expectation of anything different happening, regards Hillsborough. Another year. Another anniversary. Yet, twenty years was a landmark. The sense and feeling were that a larger than normal attendance at Anfield was expected. It was pretty much full to capacity. It turned out to be one of the most special days the famous old stadium had ever witnessed. It was not about claiming another league title, or a legendary European night, under the lights. No. This was far more important than that. The fact that a government minister was about to speak at the twentieth anniversary was something of a surprise, and a notable first. The new Culture, Media and Sport Secretary of State, Andy Burnham MP, was invited to say something to all in attendance. Not many people had heard of him, even in Labour circles. The new prime minister, Gordon Brown, had asked him to attend and deliver a speech. The faceless Blair had gone. The controversies of illegal wars, kissing Murdoch's backside and questionable cover ups, that involved eminent professors who committed suicide, took its toll. The 'war criminal' labels stuck. As did the 'weapons of mass destruction' controversy. If only people had listened to the likes of Denis Skinner. A politician with scruples, a firebrand, yes, but with integrity and honesty. There are very few politicians quite like the Beast from Bolsover.

It took an awful lot of courage, balls, guts, whatever words you use, for Andy Burnham to stand there in front of a packed Kop and face the anger of so many people. A rightful anger. The same old story of not doing anything for the 96, the families and survivors. The silence was deafening as the former MP for Leigh stood there. Then, one voice became many thousands of voices as the crowd cried out, 'Justice for the 96, justice for the 96, justice for the 96…' Andy Burnham was under no illusions what needed to happen next. It was an uncomfortable ride.

This was the first turning point. Yes, the process would be slow, time consuming, even controversial. Yet, there was finally a government minister who actually listened, cared and empathised with us. Not bad for a Bluenose!

Gordon Brown often got a bad press. The right media painted this false picture of a dour Scot, uncaring, tight fisted, and blamed the financial crisis solely at his door. Yes, he made mistakes, but so did others. A prime example were the greed driven banks and financial institutions. For me, I would say that he understood about loss and pain, given his own personal experience of grief. The fact that he asked Andy Burnham to investigate Hillsborough, says something about the man. We all know now that Blair and Brown really did not get on. They had very stark differences. Tony the Tory did anything to protect his image, including not offending Murdoch, and his crass statement around Hillsborough, stating, 'What is the point?' Well, Mr Blair, the point was Hillsborough was a national shame, an expansive cover up, and shifting the blame.

On the other side of the coin, Gordon Brown did things quietly, privately. So, as time went on, Andy Burnham started the process of finding some kind of justice for the 96. However, a few short months after the twentieth anniversary of Hillsborough, in June 2009, Andy Burnham was moved on to become the new Health Secretary of State. Crucially, he had already set the ball rolling, and kept his promise regarding Hillsborough. Within a year, a general election was called and the birth of Cameron's coalition. Now, we were totally unsure what might happen next. There was deep fear and trepidation. However, you can always count on a Tory to put his or her foot in it, with stupid, crass comments…

The new Culture Secretary was Jeremy Hunt. Yes, that's right, Hunt, not to be confused with a couple of less than complimentary four-letter words that end with the letters N T. This public school educated Tory boy from leafy Surrey, sadly, did not engage his brain rather than his mouth. On the subject of football hooliganism, he stated, 'Football is different now. Gone are the days of hooliganism, such as Heysel and Hillsborough.'

What? There was yet another politician linking Hillsborough with hooliganism. Naturally, there was a public outcry. This needed to be challenged robustly. At that particular time, I was involved in two Hillsborough groups: HFH (Hope for Hillsborough) and HJC (Hillsborough Justice Campaign). I built up strong friendships on social media. I was invited by the late Anne Williams, who lost her young son, Kevin, at Hillsborough, to travel down to London to confront Jeremy Hunt. Anne was an uncompromising campaigner, a strong character, and would never, ever give up. She undoubtedly was the real Iron Lady. When we arrived at London Euston, we met up with Dean Harris, a fellow Hillsborough survivor. I have often met up with Deano at the game, as we had seats near each other in the Kop.

Our next plan of action was to go to Jeremy Hunt's office, just a stone's throw from Trafalgar Square. A meeting had been arranged and he agreed to see us. What I felt when I met Hunt was someone who knew he had got it wrong. There were a lot of apologies, sincere or otherwise, and claims that he had read Anne Williams' superb book. The Hillsborough Independent Panel was still in its infancy, however, a couple of panel members were there that day. Both Anne and myself, as well as Dean Harris, had some suspicions about why they were there. Anne commented on this privately, stating that they were there to 'keep an eye on me'. That really would not come as a surprise. The terms of reference regarding the panel were a concern to us. Another issue that needs to be noted, is that Murdoch was a 'close friend' of Hunt. The Culture Ministry, which included the media in its remit, could be questionable in the process, and that Hunt, as head of the department, certainly had a strong conflict of interests. However, I had to revert against type, and keep quiet. For me, that was very difficult! In the end, surprise, surprise, Hunt kept his job.

There was some concern around the Hillsborough Independent Panel, and that it may be shelved or stopped. There were rumours that 'due to financial constraints' it was in the minds of cabinet ministers to put an end to it. Another excuse. Another cover up. Another miscarriage of justice. In the past, Cameron aka 'Dodgy Dave' had said, in relation to Hillsborough, 'It is like being in a dark room searching for a black cat that was never there.' His new best friend, Nick Clegg, from the Liberal Democrats, was a Sheffield MP. One would suggest that some pressure may have been put on Clegg from South Yorkshire. In the end, however, the Independent Panel stayed, which was a blessed relief to us all.

Some people often surprise you and help comes from unexpected sources. Now I am no Tory, the ideology goes against everything I stand for. The greed, privatisation, an unfair society. I am a proud socialist, I believe in strong trade unions, public services and fairness surrounding tax, wealth and provision. When Cameron appointed Theresa May as Home Secretary, I really was not impressed. I saw her as a glamorous version of Thatcher. It seemed she was more interested in how many pairs of heels she could wear, rather than law and order policies. However, she did confront the bullying boys in blue. In the era of austerity, she made cuts to the police service. Of course, this caused to annoy the Police Federation and she faced the wrath of that particular organisation. She was the daughter of a Church of England vicar, so there was a certain degree of fairness running through her veins. Of course, certain interested parties, whether they were senior police officers, certain politicians, even judges and lawyers, were far from happy. A surprising ally had come to the fore. Furthermore, what would happen in future months and years, would send shockwaves to the whole country. I am not saying everything she said regards Hillsborough was good. For example, her statement on personally getting justice over Hillsborough was an unfortunate turn of phrase and not wholly accurate. There were many good people who did excellent work regarding Hillsborough, with many not recognised.

Chapter Nine

The Hillsborough Independent Panel Report

When the Hillsborough Independent Panel finally got the go ahead, a few key questions needed to be addressed. Who would sit on the panel? Who would be its chair? Where would it be held? What were the aims, objectives, limitations and scope of the panel?

For so long, the Hillsborough families and survivors had been shafted, disbelieved, mocked, criticised and accused, regarding the disaster. There had been the Taylor Report, the shameful original inquests, the disgraceful judicial review and the contemptible private prosecutions. There was one underlying common theme: cover up.

Each and every time, those families and survivors showed amazing determination, dignity, bravery and steel resolve against the system, that cannot be underestimated and can only be praised beyond comparison. Naturally, we still feared the worst. All those setbacks had taken their toll. From the outset, everything was against us. The day following the tragedy, the so-called 'elite' gathered on the broken, crumbling terrace of Leppings Lane. They were all there: Thatcher, Hurd, Ingham, representing politicians, Duckenfield, Murray, Wright, Middup from South Yorkshire Police, Kelly from the FA and Mackrell from Sheffield Wednesday, amongst others. The elite? A more appropriate and accurate description would be of a bunch of lying sewer rats.

So, where do we start with the Hillsborough Independent Panel? On 28th January 2010, The Guardian wrote:

'It has emerged that the Hillsborough Independent Panel will meet every month in Liverpool. It will be chaired by the Very Reverend James Jones, the Anglican Bishop of Liverpool. The panel members will include Professor Phil Scraton from Queens University, Belfast, a leading authority on the tragedy. Others will include renowned journalist and broadcaster, Peter Sissons, Doctor Bill Kirkup, who will offer his medical expertise. A television producer and investigative journalist, Katy Jones, who worked on Jimmy McGovern's excellent Hillsborough docudrama, will also work on the panel...'

This would be the basis of the panel, and what they may or may not investigate. Yet, it was perfectly clear that something monumental could be on the cards. Possibly. If you looked at who was on the panel, it certainly gave some degree of optimism. On that basis, what would those, who many thought were ultimately responsible for Hillsborough, think about the whole affair? It would not take much working out. It would also take almost three years of investigations to finally reveal the conclusions. The remit of the panel that was set out within the terms of reference were:

- Oversee public disclosure
- Consult with the Hillsborough families

- Manage the process of public disclosure
- Establish an archive of Hillsborough documentation
- Produce a report to explain the work of the panel

This is just a brief summary of the details. It is available in great detail through the HMSO (Her Majesty's Stationery Office).

One vital intervention was when Andy Burnham MP was still Culture Secretary, he implemented an order to change the rules on the time when government records were made available in the public domain. This was very much a key decision that went in the Hillsborough campaigners' favour. Something seemed to go right for a change.

If we look into the brief background, and the history of Hillsborough, it does make some interesting reading. The stadium was built in 1899, and was often chosen as the venue for FA Cup semi-finals as a neutral ground. It was often selected as its location, outside the city centre by around four miles, would be 'easy to manage'. Another factor was the transport links with favourable access. However, in the 1980s, when hooliganism was at its sickening height, and crowd control was more desirable than crowd safety, there were a few near fatal incidents and missed opportunities. Yet, none of this had anything to do with bad behaviour or crowd disorder. It was crowd safety that was the main concern.

There were four FA Cup semi-finals held at Hillsborough in the 1980s. In 1981, Tottenham Hotspur played Wolverhampton Wanderers. It has been noted by many Spurs fans regarding the serious nature of crushing at the

Leppings Lane end. There were a number of injuries but thankfully, no fatalities. There was a gap of some six years before the next FA Cup semi-final was played at Hillsborough, between Coventry City and Leeds United. It was 'very uncomfortable' according to Leeds fans in Leppings Lane. The next two FA Cup semi-finals, in 1988 and 1989, involved both Liverpool and Nottingham Forest. As we all know, tragedy was about to befall LFC in 1989. Again, the warning signs were there. The same scenario. Injury, Leppings Lane and real fear. I was there in 1988. It was unbearably tight, uncomfortable and quite frightening. I was in one of the side pens, and believe me, I was glad to get out of that situation. A year later, I was back there and the living hell of Hillsborough was witnessed by the whole country...

In gathering evidence, the Hillsborough Independent Panel left no stone unturned. The process was long, complicated and time-consuming. It had to be if the *real* truth was to be uncovered. After all, the families and survivors had waited for over twenty years to get some kind of justice, but time and again they were let down by the system and the people in power. They could wait a little longer, despite the frustrations and the seemingly endless wait for justice.

Anyone who has read the Hillsborough Independent Panel Report, either online or with a hard copy, will realise what a complex and time-consuming document it really is. Therefore, I have had to be extremely selective in informing readers of the subject matter and the interpretation. The following is a brief synopsis of the work of the panel and their investigations. Naturally, there were those who would not cooperate with investigations, and I would imagine that anyone who has even the briefest knowledge of Hillsborough would readily know who I am talking about. I would like to refer to several key issues regarding Hillsborough as a 'safe venue', when, in reality, it was 'not fit for purpose'. There was also the frosty relationship between Sheffield Wednesday Football Club and South Yorkshire Police. Not to mention the failure to follow recommendations in the Green Guide, as regards to spectator safety. It was a case of blind ignorance.

If you dig deep enough, you uncover much. This was the case with Hillsborough. The painstaking research and wading through of many thousands of documents, more than 400,000 to be precise, would bear much fruit. When the days became weeks, and the months became years, it was quite clear that something significant would eventually play out. The panel had been at it for almost three years, starting in February 2010. However, a date was finally set where the panel would reveal its conclusions. A monumental day that was etched on the minds of everyone connected to Hillsborough, the city of Liverpool and LFC itself. Truth day: 12th September 2012.

Chapter Ten

Truth Day: 12th September 2012

There are certain days that stay with you for the rest of your life. Well, Thursday 12th September 2012 was one of those days. It was a day with many mixed emotions, tears of joy, moments of sadness, reflection. For the city of Liverpool, it was a pivotal day in its long and rich history. Liverpool is a city like no other. A city that has had to fight for its own identity, even respect. A city that is culturally diverse, and has more of a continental feel. There is a saying, emblazoned on badges and T-shirts: Scouse Not English. This is something that we are deeply proud of. It is perfectly true to state that we have more in common with our Celtic neighbours: Ireland, Scotland, Wales. The English? Well, a minor irritation if truth be told. We are a deeply socialist city, fiercely independent, and of course, have a deep love of football.

I set off early doors by train, to Liverpool Lime Street. It was a shocking day weather wise, it never stopped raining. After a couple of jars, I headed into town and ended up at The Bridewell, which was a former police station that housed a number of police cells. It was now a pub. It was close to the Anglican Cathedral, where the Hillsborough Independent Panel would release the much anticipated report. I decided to 'camp' there, at The Bridewell.

I waited, nervously, still not knowing what the outcome would be. I calmed my nerves with a few bevvies. I watched news coverage of the day, waiting patiently for updates.

A few people came and went. I met up with a fellow Hillsborough survivor, Gareth O'Leary, who had been up to the cathedral. Of course, by this point, things had started to become clear. After more than three years of intensive investigations, that involved the processing of over a million documents, the real truth of Hillsborough had finally been revealed. We were right all along. They lied. It was all over the media, specifically on TV news and the radio. It was *the* story, and it dominated the air time. I wondered as I reflected on what The S*n would think about it all. They would probably lie through their teeth and create smears and myths, just like they did in 1989. Naturally, the families and survivors were triumphant in one sense, but also reflective. It had taken twenty-three years just to get to this point, but there was still more to be done. Much more.

As crowds gathered, the rain continued to fall. There was a certain buzz around Lime Street and Saint George's Hall. There was raw emotion and a certain vibrancy. This was undoubtedly a very special day. As we milled around, we were approached by BBC Radio 5 Live, asking for an interview. Both Gareth and myself agreed. Now, I have to admit that I don't have a face for TV. Radio, maybe. I am not what you would call 'photogenic'. We did the interview, getting our strong points across to the public. All in all, it went well.

We saw the prime minister's statement in parliament on TV where he talked about 'a double injustice' in regards to Hillsborough. How times had changed. Gone were the days when he stated that Hillsborough was like 'searching for a black cat in a dark room that was never there'.

What the Hillsborough Independent Panel Report stated sent shockwaves around the country and beyond. The mass cover up was brutally exposed, as were the blatant lies and disgraceful smears. The Hillsborough Independent Panel Report is a massive document, some 400 pages long. What I will divulge here is just a mere glimpse of what was published, which I will now explain in brief, salient points.

Crowd Safety

It was perfectly clear that the safety of those who were at Hillsborough was severely compromised and that control replaced safety. At every level, this caused the catastrophic situation to develop. Access to the bottleneck of Leppings Lane to the turnstiles, which were inadequate and of poor condition. The mismanagement of the crowd by SYP and the stewards, alterations to the terrace, the condition and placement of barriers and the construction of the pens, access to the central pens through the antiquated tunnel with a 6:1 gradient and poor lighting. Such deficiencies were known to those in charge.

Operational Failings

The fatal flaws concentrated on crowd disorder, almost to an obsession. This was highlighted with police and stewards who operated such a mindset. Instead of focusing on safety and care, it was all about drink, ticketlessness and hooliganism. In respect of all three, they were not contributory factors. There were fatal mistakes, many, such as the failure to recognise overcrowding and the build-up of fans around the concourse, the failure to recognise the opening of exit gates to relieve congestion, the failure to manage the pens effectively, the absolutely unbelievable decision not to seal the tunnel to the central pens and the obvious incompetence to not evaluate the situation that was nothing to do with disorder, but was everything to do with overcrowding. The crass decision to offer the role of match commander to an inexperienced senior officer, who had never been in charge of an important, high-profile match before, showed the contempt shown by SYP hierarchy.

The Emergency Response

As for the emergency response, which was viewed as 'chaotic', the number of severe casualties was not acted upon properly, the activation of a major incident plan was very poor, and proved very limited. As a direct failure, the leadership response was not what should have been expected in such a situation. As a result, rescue and recovery efforts were severely hampered. The triage policy adopted, as well as use of vital equipment, together with lack of coordination, was unhelpful, to say the least.

The emergency response had not been previously examined at Hillsborough. This was down to false assumptions that those who had died had already been fixed, and that the notion was that they could no longer have been helped. The report stated that whilst it was not possible to state that any individual lives could have been saved, it is clear based on evidence given to the panel, that some victims, if they had been given help with vital equipment, vital support could then have been administered with the potential to save more lives.

The Medical Evidence

During the inquests, the coroner ruled that all who had died had done so by 3:15 p.m., and that cut-off point had been adopted. In relating to medical evidence, it was argued that those who died did so by the 3:15 time frame. The panel had access to data that confirmed the notion that a single and rapid pattern of death was unsustainable. Some of those who died did so after a significant period of unconsciousness. Therefore, some individuals had the potential to survive. On the basis of documented evidence, and the fact that some victims had a degree of partial recovery from asphyxiation, it cannot be concluded that death had occurred prior to 3:15 p.m.

Deflection of Blame

It is perfectly clear that South Yorkshire Police had an agenda from the start to blame Liverpool fans. They established a case regarding drink, ticketlessness and unruly and aggressive behaviour. Some eight years after the disaster, it was revealed publicly for the first time, that handwritten recollections were altered, redacted, doctored and changed by senior police officers and the force solicitors. Some 116 out of 164 statements were tampered with.

The Headlines

The panel investigated the newspaper and media coverage around Hillsborough. Naturally, a lot of it focused on the role of The S*n and its association with South Yorkshire Police and the Police Federation in Sheffield. A local MP was also in the mix, as was a Sheffield news agency. Evidence supported that a false narrative, and a shifting the blame policy was adopted. The panel found no significant evidence to support the claim of drunkenness, ticketlessness or unruly behaviour.

Thursday 12th September 2012 was a day that will forever be etched on my memory. It was charged with electrifying emotion, filled with tears and much, much more. It was easy to forget the rain. In the evening, we listened to the powerful speeches. I was standing opposite Saint George's Hall, a stone's throw from Liverpool Lime

Street. It would be handy to catch the train later on. The crowds gathered and soon it was just a sea of humanity, roads closed off, the crowd expectant. This was a moment to be a proud Liverpudlian. A moment that exposed the myths, the smears, the lies, the vile coverage, the corruption, the cover ups and proved that they lied.

The future would involve other days in court. For today, however, this was the families' day, the survivors' day, a day for the 96. It was truth day.

Chapter Eleven

Goodnight and God Bless, Dad

Robert Whittle
15th January 1920—8th November 2013

Around the same time as truth day, my dad started to become unwell. He was ninety-three years old, and as the saying goes, 'as fit as a fiddle'. He had a very interesting life with some tragedy, it must be said. His own father, Yates Whittle, was a war hero, serving on the Western Front throughout the First World War. He took part in many decisive battles, including the Somme. I never met my grandfather, but heard a lot of stories about him. He was a private in the Queen's Lancashire Regiment, 2nd Battalion. You could probably imagine the horrors he faced in the so-called 'Great War'. He came back a broken man, suffering from 'shellshock' that is now known as PTSD or post-traumatic stress disorder. When he went to war, he was a teetotal. When he came back, he was a drunk. That is what war does to you. Sadly, his life was torn apart through drink, womanising and petty theft. My grandfather never really recovered.

My dad, Robert Whittle, excelled at school, under the teaching of legendary filmmaker and local historian, Sam Hanna. He then became a draughtsman, then chief draughtsman, at Bank Hall Colliery, in Burnley. He spent some thirty-five years at the pit before its closure in the early 1970s. In those days, the pits provided guaranteed employment, almost for life. My dad was offered work at other pits, but decided for a change. He applied to a teacher training college and studied at Alsager, in Cheshire. After successfully completing the training, a post was offered to him at Norden High School, in Rishton, near Blackburn. My dad stayed there up to his retirement in 1985.

A long, healthy retirement followed, for almost thirty years. Of course, there were moments of deep hurt, notably my late brother's death in 1994, as well as the tragedy of Hillsborough in 1989; my family not knowing if I was alive or dead. These very traumatic events can affect you at any time, but to be elderly and retired, it really does hit home. I think that is why two or three years after Anthony, my dad suffered from bowel cancer. The immense stress of what he had to endure, as well as a shocking, horrific death, and the loss of his youngest son, took its toll on him. On all of us.

It was a Sunday morning in early December. I had gone to attend Mass, like I did most Sundays. I had this eerie sensation of deep dread. I thought nothing of it at first. Sometimes you get those horrible feelings in the pit of your stomach. A sheer emptiness, a thought of déjà vu. All very weird, like it transcends reality. I just had to rush home. Something was very, very wrong. I didn't even go to the house. I went straight to the hospital, which is just across a busy main road. I got to A & E (Accident and Emergency). My fears were soon realised.

It was explained to me that my dad had been in intense pain and had passed out a number of times. He had been in and out of crash on a couple of occasions. A consultant told us there may be a small lump and my dad was transferred to a ward for investigations. Naturally, it was a tense time for the family. A couple of days later, an operation was performed by an absolutely brilliant surgeon. A lump had been removed and the rest of the bowels were clear. A blessed relief. My dad had almost another twenty years of good health.

His final year was a difficult one. He did not seem to be himself, and was often tired. What can you expect at over ninety years of age? We called our GP and he was misdiagnosed. The fact that my dad had an obvious yellow-orange colour to his face, as if he had been in the sun too long, should have been recognised by the doctor. It was obvious jaundice, and a possible problem with the gallbladder. Another doctor came and we were advised to take him to Royal Blackburn Hospital. My dad spent the last year of his life in a hospital bed. Some of the treatment he received was shocking and appalling. However, there were also outstanding levels of care from many doctors and nurses. We went there every day for over twelve months. It was a rollercoaster ride at times. There were good days, bad days, setbacks and some glimpses of hope. Even aged ninety-three, my dad had to endure a long and complex operation. Initial signs were good, and we were told the procedure was successful. However, it transpired that a large mass had been found in the gallbladder. When the consultant finally got around to see us, he told us my dad would not get better. We were given the shocking news of the fact he had about three months left to live. But my dad, being Dad, lasted around twice as long. He was a supreme fighter. He did sleep a lot more and struggled with food. Naturally, he lost a lot of weight. As he slowly slipped away, I was thankful that he would have a quiet, peaceful death. As a Eucharistic Minister, I was able to give my dad the Sacrament of the Sick and Holy Communion. It was a supreme blessing.

Come mid to late October, it was decided my dad would be transferred to a nursing home. Letting him slip away in a hospital bed was very upsetting, to say the least. I wanted somewhere for my dad to be comfortable and peaceful in what time he had left. With my wife Deborah's help, we got him transferred to Dove Court Nursing Home, in Burnley. Deborah is a senior sister and unit manager there, so the transfer was not a problem. He had a lovely, warm, comfortable room, overlooking the garden. We knew he would not be there very long, maybe a couple of weeks. Yet, he was at peace.

On Thursday night, 7th November, we were in Blackpool as a family. We had other family members who knew how to contact us if we had to return home in an emergency. In the evening, we got an urgent call that we needed to return home immediately. It was time.

The car journey was truly horrible. I don't know how I managed to do that drive, but I did. I was just hoping that we got back in time, before my dad passed. There were a lot of things that swirled around inside my head. A crazy PTSD moment engulfed me. My fears were very profound and meaningful. I just had to see my dad one last time. Thankfully, we made it. I parked up in the car park and headed to the unit where my dad was. Both Deborah and myself went to the room. My mum was there, along with Deborah's parents, Paul and Doris. We could see that Dad was conscious, but seemingly did not recognise us. The breathing was, as yet, not shallow. Deborah and myself stayed for a while…

In the early hours of the morning, Dove Court contacted us. It was time. The breathing was shallow and increasingly so. My dad was slowly, painlessly, slipping away. The point of death was there. He just breathed his last breath. A happy, peaceful, dignified death. A long ninety-three years of life. Much accomplished. Many rewards. There were times of happiness, sadness, heartache and joy. He would be with Anthony now.

Farewell, Dad. Goodbye 'Our Bob'. A life well lived.

Chapter Twelve

Monica Rose

There are times that are bittersweet. There are also times when you have to journey along the crossroads of life.

A few short weeks after my father's death, and a week before Christmas Day, a magical, precious gift came into our lives. The date was 17th December 2013. The birth of our beautiful granddaughter, Monica Rose. My Monica Moo. We had all hoped my dad would have seen his great granddaughter born. Sadly, it was not to be. A mere five weeks between death and life.

Yet, we had a new chapter in our life: Monica. I had to put all my focus on my little princess. Undoubtedly, she changed my life. She was the best thing that ever happened to me, that was without question. She gave my life meaning and a purpose. The first day I held her was the day she melted my heart. From that day, we have had a strong, unbreakable bond.

A lot of my life has centred around my faith, and Saint John the Baptist Roman Catholic Church in Burnley, Lancashire. I was there, virtually from birth. There have been baptisms, confirmation, first Holy Communions, as well as weddings and funerals, even memorial services. This very faith has answered my questions, especially in those darkest days. There was a light there that guided me, rescued me, revitalised me. A spirit of living waters that refreshed me. A small tree that blossomed, to bear much fruit. I doubt whether I would be here today if I had not reaffirmed my faith.

I have been involved in several parish occasions, whether it was Requiem Masses, a Nuptial Mass or a baptism. There were differing emotions. To immerse yourself in faith is a very rewarding and fulfilling experience. Everything revolved around faith, despite the fact that I became lapsed as regards to the church. Like a lot of teenagers, I could not recognise, or indeed grasp the fact, that faith had some relevance in my life. When you are sixteen, you have other needs or wants, even desires. You rebel, you turn away. I turned away for seventeen years. I did not have anyone to guide me. It was no coincidence that during those years, I had a lot of baggage that I carried around with me. A lot of negativity, making the wrong choices, doing shameful things. Whether it was problem relationships, drinking, violence, or a police record.

The two most horrific moments in my life—Hillsborough in 1989 and my brother's death in 1994—hit me when I was away from church. As I have already stated, my need for prayer came the day after Anthony's death. I have often regretted not being led back to my faith, following Hillsborough. I was emotionally being ripped apart; my soul eaten away inside. A huge amount of anger manifested itself, and all the dark demons of PTSD just about destroyed me.

As the years rolled by, my faith grew stronger. I got involved in a number of church ministries, becoming almost part of the furniture! The sense of belonging and developing my faith certainly helped me cope with everyday life. It was just very small things, and it certainly was not one gigantic vision on the road to Damascus. Far from it, but it was there. The involvement in parish life, the companionship, the togetherness and the growth spiritually, was the key to a previously bolted door, with no hope of entry. Whether it was just attending Mass, or becoming a Eucharistic Minister, a welcomer, involved in various church programmes such as Journey in Faith, Holy Spirit Days or a member of the Parish Bereavement Team, helped to mould me and overcome struggles.

As Monica grew and developed, she too became part of the Saint John's furniture. The other parishioners loved her to bits, and were wowed with her bright personality and radiant smile. She is a very special character. To take her to church is a wonderful experience, and is a real honour and privilege. We often go to what is known as the Little Church, where children learn about our Catholic faith in a way that keeps them interested. Monica actually loves going there and her grumpy old grandad is only too happy to take her! She has followed in my footsteps by attending the same primary school that is linked to the church: Saint John the Baptist. Everything has gone full circle. I really did not think that my life would have been such a treasure, an unbelievable gift from Christ.

Monica had a difficult start in life. So, it was up to us, meaning my wife, Deborah, and myself, to grasp the nettles as it were. It was true to state that Monica was an unexpected gift. Yet, we would never criticise or condemn our daughter. We are not like that. We were there to fully support her no matter what. There were difficult times ahead. However, I will not go into that, a private and deeply personal family matter. All that I will say is that I had to take up the role of carer and babysitter, virtually since Monica's birth. It is a role that I have relished, and it really was something that made me. All through her early years, the so-called 'terrible twos', through to nursery, and then onto primary school, I was there. Naturally, I did not get everything right but you do learn from your mistakes. I have also brought Monica up properly, in a footballing sense. She is a true Red, a natural Kopite, and has even been to a number of games. In many ways, this is her real education, and without blowing my own trumpet, she has had a good tutor!

Chapter Thirteen

The New Inquests:
Truth and Justice?

Following the monumental victory after the Hillsborough Independent Panel Report was published on 12th September 2012, the desire to quash the original inquests was strong. This was going to be the obvious next step. To overturn the original 'accidental death' verdicts was a necessity, a right, and the next step towards justice. Given what was proven by the panel, it was the only possible course of action. However, after so many years of fighting the system, huge setbacks, deliberate delays and excuse after excuse, the families and survivors were naturally cautious and even sceptical about future outcomes.

Surprisingly, things moved relatively quickly. In December 2012, some four months after the Hillsborough Independent Panel Report was published, the Attorney General, Dominic Grieve, decided that following the panel report, he was going to apply to the High Court to quash the original inquest verdicts, and that new inquests be ordered. In the eyes of the law, those inquests did not exist, and the new inquests would look at the evidence again. This was a very positive moment. Now, I am no Tory, but I can happily applaud Dominic Grieve and his decision to order new inquests. Of course, not everyone was going to be happy about it, certainly not in South Yorkshire.

The new inquests started on 31st March 2014, and would be the longest ever in British legal history. There was much debate on where the inquests would be held. For obvious reasons, Sheffield was quickly ruled out, as was Liverpool, the argument being that there may be accusations of bias from certain interested individuals and parties. There were popular venues around the north west of England, notably in Lancashire and Cheshire. The rumour mills suggested Preston, Wigan or Warrington. In the end, the most favourable option was Warrington. The inquests would be held on a modern industrial estate at Birchwood Park, in a unit that was specially built to house a state of the art courtroom. The inquests concluded on 26th April 2016, just over two years later.

It was a long, drawn out affair. For two years, the bereaved families and survivors had steadfastly gone to court, almost daily in many cases. There were a lot of individuals who were either seriously unwell or of older age, and had to listen to testimonies that were particularly graphic, as well as deeply offensive and filled with lies and smears. Some things hadn't changed and false narratives, blatant lies and fabrications were still abound. It was pitiful behaviour with no remorse whatsoever. My thoughts were conflicted in the sense that I could not comprehend the thought of those who I felt as responsible would get away with it, again. Yet, on the other side of the coin, I could tell myself that maybe this time, there would be justice.

So, why did the new inquests take so long? Obviously, a case of this magnitude, together with many interested parties, would take time to conclude. However, the ongoing refusal of South Yorkshire Police and others, to accept responsibility, to continually blame fans, a rigid determination to follow strict guidelines of drink, ticketlessness, late arrivals and unruly behaviour, did, without doubt, delay the proceedings quite markedly. Of course, they were helped by certain barristers who expanded on those vile myths and smears. It certainly felt like the longest two years in our lives.

You need to delve into the processes of the new inquests to get a distinct flavour and a deep understanding of those inquests. A major failure of the original inquests was the now infamous decision by the coroner, Stefan Popper, not to allow evidence beyond 3:15 p.m. This crass decision implemented by the original coroner would have a damaging and long lasting impact on the disaster. There was no investigation in relation to the time of death, and whether or not those victims had the potential to survive. Furthermore, there was no indication of acceptance of omissions from the emergency response. The impact of Popper's decision could not be more damning. The short-sighted insistence was not only questionable, but undoubtedly led to the grossly inappropriate recording of accidental death.

Of course, the most unpalatable process of the original inquests was the damning and deliberately callous interpretation of falsehood regarding police statements. The alteration and amendments were shocking, to say the least. A total of 116 out of 164 statements were changed, altered, amended or redacted. The original inquests were dominated with the police peddling the same old smear-led myths that focused on drink and alcohol consumption, a false assertion of fans without tickets, late arrival of fans and an unruly mob intent on trouble. The original inquests were supposed to establish how the loved ones had died at Hillsborough. That is what inquests do. It is not a criminal trial. So, why was it that the families felt they were being accused? Why did they think they were actually on trial? Why did they feel they were being condemned? It was a disgraceful mockery of cover up to protect vested self-interests. It was an absolute travesty. It was an orchestrated fit up.

In returning to the second Hillsborough inquests, which began on 31st March 2014, there were some 4,000 documents and 500 witnesses. The jury consisted of six women and three men. The vast gathering of evidence was an extremely daunting task to undertake. The jurors, to their immense credit, were not swayed or taken in by the police barristers, or their odious lies. They were still peddling the same old discredited and blatant lies, smears and myths around drink, ticketless fans, time of arrival and a notion of bad behaviour. It is important to state that the barrister central to all of this was John Beggs QC. His profile made for interesting reading that stated, 'the man to contact when the police are in trouble'. Due to such crass behaviour, this is one of the main reasons why the inquests took over two years to complete. The indisputable fact that South Yorkshire Police and SYMAS (South

Yorkshire Metropolitan Ambulance Service) fought tirelessly, like tooth and nail, to continually press home the false narratives that had already been devalued and were a complete pack of lies, was not lost on the jury either.

What the families were striving for was when Duckenfield would appear at the inquests to give his 'evidence'. On 9th March 2015, they got their wish. His evidence lasted six days. Duckenfield said he was 'under pressure' as the disaster unfolded. Surely, a senior police officer, with the rank of chief superintendent, would be able to deal with such pressure? Of course, you could say, on the other side of the coin, that he was out of his depth and had no big match experience. The fact he was given the job by the chief constable, possibly due to associations with the local Masonic Lodge, was a fatal error. However, ultimate responsibility was with Duckenfield. Those six days in court at the second inquest, was when *finally* Duckenfield admitted fault, liability, blame, and that lie was, at long last, admitted by a very cowardly man. The first day, Duckenfield admitted he was 'probably not the right man for the job'. Day two, he stated that failing to recognise the consequences of opening the exit gates was 'the biggest regret of my life'. Then came the startling admission that he *had* lied about moments after the tragedy had unfolded regarding the exit gate and his conversation with Graham Kelly of the FA. He stated he would 'regret that lie until his dying day'. He concluded that he could not deny 'that the decision not to close off the tunnel was a blunder of the first magnitude'. Yet, Duckenfield refused to say that it was 'gross negligence'. He finally accepted that 'failure to close off the tunnel was the direct result of 96 deaths at Hillsborough'.

The families listened intently to Duckenfield's evidence. It was an extremely difficult and traumatic situation to endure. I watched the news coverage on TV. I really wished I could have been there, but unfortunately, sadly, I was still in a very dark place. I managed to attend the inquests, just for one day. I have to admit, it was a difficult thing to do. Yet, as I watched the coverage, I felt great pride as I heard the interview with Barry Devonside, a prominent family member who lost his beautiful son, Christopher, at Hillsborough. Barry confronted Duckenfield outside the court. It was the same predictable, cowardly squirming of a man who fed on lies, fabrication and cover up. As for Mr Devonside, I salute you, Barry. You are one wonderful, deeply committed and brave individual. God bless you. YNWA.

When it came to the verdicts, I did not get a wink of sleep the night before; not many did. It was one of those stressed-out, stomach-churning moments that we all fear. A lot of 'what if' moments swirled around inside my head. I just had to wait until the verdicts were announced or returned. My eyes were intently glued to the TV, as I watched the BBC news channel.

The day itself, 26th April 2016, was a monumental day. The coverage cannot be faulted. It dominated the news for most of the day. It was fronted by the BBC's Ben Brown, who is actually a Liverpool fan, though was very much an impartial observer. He was assisted by the BBC legal expert, Clive Coleman. The jury were instructed to answer fourteen questions related to the tragedy, including one that focused on crowd behaviour. During the two-year inquests, barristers representing police officers, maliciously rammed home the deliberate falsehoods, smears and fabrication.

When the jury returned its findings, they could be no more damning, and who was clearly to blame. They had to answer fourteen questions in order to reach their verdict.

Question One

Do you agree with the following statement that 96 people died as a result of a disaster at the Hillsborough football stadium, on 15th April 1989, due to crushing in the central pens of the Leppings Lane terrace, following the admission of a large number of supporters to the stadium through an exit gate?

Answer recorded: yes.

Question Two

Was there any error or omission in police planning and operation for the FA Cup semi-final, on 15th April 1989, which caused or contributed to the dangerous situation which developed during the match?

Answer recorded: yes.

Question Three

Was there any error or omission in policing on the day of the match which caused and contributed to a dangerous situation developing at the Leppings Lane turnstiles?

Answer recorded: yes.

Question Four
Was there any error or omission from commanding officers which caused or contributed to the crush on the terrace?
    Answer recorded: yes.

Question Five
When the order was given to open the exit gates at the Leppings Lane end of the stadium, was there any error or omission by the commanding officers in the control box which caused or contributed to the crush on the terrace?
    Answer recorded: yes.

Question Six
Are you satisfied, that you can be absolutely sure, that those who died in the disaster were unlawfully killed?
    Answer recorded: yes.

Question Seven
Was there any behaviour by supporters that caused or contributed to the dangerous situation at the turnstiles?
    Answer recorded: no.

Question Eight
Were there any features of the design, construction and layout of the stadium which you consider dangerous or defective, and which caused or contributed to the disaster?
    Answer recorded: yes.

Question Nine

Was there any error or omission in the safety certification and oversight of Hillsborough Stadium that caused and contributed to the disaster?

Answer recorded: yes.

Question Ten

Was there any error or omission by Sheffield Wednesday and its staff in the management of the stadium and/or preparation for the semi-final match on 15th April 1989, which caused or contributed to the disaster?

Answer recorded: yes.

Question Eleven

Was there any error or omission by Sheffield Wednesday and its staff on 15th April 1989, which caused or contributed to the dangerous situation that developed at the Leppings Lane turnstiles or on the west terrace?

Answer recorded: no.

Question Twelve

Should Eastwood & Partners, the structural engineers, have done more to detect and advise on any unsafe and unsatisfactory features of the Hillsborough stadium that could have caused or contributed to the disaster?

Answer recorded: yes.

Question Thirteen

After the crush had started to develop in the west terrace, was there any error or omission by the police which caused or contributed to losses of life in the disaster?

Answer recorded: yes.

Question Fourteen

After the crush had started to develop in the west terrace, was there any error or omission by the ambulance service, SYMAS, which caused or contributed to losses of life in the disaster?

Answer recorded: yes.

As you can probably imagine, I had very mixed emotions on that remarkable day, 26th April 2016. There was joy, sadness, anger, hurt, pain and relief. It had been a long and deeply troubling journey that had taken the majority of my adult life, a life that controlled me through darkness and fear. However, I was not the only one. There were so many survivors and bereaved families who struggled to come to terms with it all. The grief, the accusations, the smears, the condemnation. Sadly, it took so many people to the grave. There were those who never recovered emotionally. There were some who could not simply take anymore. There were those who suffered failing health as a direct result of Hillsborough. There were many more than 97 deaths at Hillsborough. These were the forgotten victims of Hillsborough. We will always honour the 97 angels, of that there is absolutely no doubt. They are never forgotten. We will always remember them, pray for them, think of them. They will always be in our hearts.

As the second Hillsborough inquest concluded, the disgraceful accidental death verdicts from the flawed original inquests had been wiped away. The new verdict of unlawful killing was not only a blessed relief, it was something that should have been recorded more than a quarter of a century before. As the most famous football anthem, 'You'll Never Walk Alone', was sung outside the courtroom with much raw emotional energy in a mixture of tears and joy, the families and survivors present had got there after many years of struggle, setbacks, delays, heartache and pain. On a personal note, I was ecstatic and reflective. I wished fervently I had been there. It was truly emotional. Hillsborough touched my life like nothing else. It had now gone full circle. Those words, 'truth and justice' ring true. However, was there *real* truth and justice?

Chapter Fourteen

Operation Unresolved

Following the new inquests, and the unlawfully killed verdicts, the next obvious step was to progress with criminal proceedings. The breadth of the investigation within the scope of Operation Resolve was a wide ranging and complex one. Not only were there plans to prosecute senior actors involved in the Hillsborough disaster, it also was to investigate survivors' evidence, in which investigators visited my home. I played it very safe, by inviting my local Roman Catholic priest along to bear witness to what I was about to say. The investigators, two females, actually agreed to my request to have a witness present. They stayed for almost two hours. I had to look through masses of photographs that focused on the outer concourse, the concertina gates, the wall by the river and Leppings Lane itself. I then had to give a lengthy and precise statement regarding the day. It was a difficult and stressful task to undertake. However, I got through it.

The CPS (Crown Prosecution Service) were involved in the process of setting up any cases that warranted a prosecution. In conjunction with Operation Resolve, any relevant evidence would be processed and if the CPS agreed there was sufficient evidence, then they would sanction a case to proceed. The indisputable fact was that former Chief Superintendent David Duckenfield would be charged on ninety-five counts of gross negligence manslaughter. It was ninety-five counts, as Tony Bland survived for several years, with PVS (persistent vegetative state). There were a few others, including Graham Mackrell, the club chief executive, and shockingly, the designated safety officer at Sheffield Wednesday. Also, Donald Denton, another former senior officer; Alan Foster, his assistant; Peter Metcalf, the former solicitor for the South Yorkshire force, and last but not least, one Sir Norman Bettison, chief inspector with South Yorkshire Police at the time of the disaster, who organised a so-called 'Black Ops' smear campaign. This was before he got the job of chief constable, with both Merseyside Police and the West Yorkshire force. Of course, Bettison received a knighthood for his 'police service'. A very sick joke. He then became a writer of 'fantasy fiction'. For all the years of hell, disgraceful lies, fabrication and falsehood, corruptible practices and costing the lives of 97 innocent men, women and children, of families torn apart in unbearable grief, survivors left traumatised and being blamed falsely, injured victims in their thousands, unable to cope or exist, it came down to just six men being charged. It really did stick in the throat.

At that point, of course, it was all about successfully getting convictions for those being accused. There were good, positive days over the past few years, with the Hillsborough Independent Panel Report and the second inquests. Finally, we were being listened to and getting some kind of justice. What transpired gave some comfort and peace for the families and survivors. The blind arrogance and disgraceful denials were plain to see. When it was decided that the trial was set, and the venue chosen, namely Preston Crown Court, it was a case of here we go again. This time, we honestly thought, *justice at last.*

The absolute iron clad fact is that Duckenfield, who was charged with ninety-five counts of gross negligence manslaughter, should have meant guilty verdicts all the way. You cannot be found not guilty with so many counts, especially when the second inquests proved as much. You have to dig deep and see the tangled web of deceit. Certain corruptible practices were at play. Firstly, there was Duckenfield, the Freemason. Then there were former police officers under the guise of Operation Resolve. The 'old pals act' came into play. Furthermore, there was the woefully ineffective and institutionally corrupt Crown Prosecution Service. At that time, it was under the 'leadership' of the odious Alison Saunders, the Director of Public Prosecutions, who was always against the families and survivors of Hillsborough. There was no chance whatsoever that she would allow for justice to be served. Moreover, this woman disgracefully failed the family in the Stephen Lawrence case. She failed in procedures of several rape cases. Then there was Hillsborough. To rub salt into the wounds, she was given a gong from the Queen for 'good service to the judicial system'. When she was found out, she returned it to save face. Unbelievable. Now, she works for a high-profile law firm, Linklaters. Disgusting beyond belief.

The scene was set, Preston Crown Court was the venue for the trial of Duckenfield, and that of Mackrell, the former club secretary/chief executive of Sheffield Wednesday Football Club. The trial would last six weeks and the jury would deliberate for many hours but were unable to reach a verdict. There was a retrial set, in a relatively quick turnaround. Again, it was Preston Crown Court. Again, it was the openly biased, and disgraceful judge, Sir Peter Openshaw. Is it little wonder that there is no respect, and no public confidence in the judicial process?

When the retrial began, on 7th October, Openshaw took his place in the courtroom, as did Duckenfield, but was given the privilege to sit in the bowels of the court. There was no ignominy of being paraded as the accused on trial. It was blindly obvious that favours were made and that Duckenfield was treated more like a VIP than a prisoner. Everyone knew that he was part of the Black Hand Gang or the Freemasons. Now I do not know if Openshaw was or is a Freemason, but I would hazard a guess that he probably was. They stick together like mud when they need to help each other out. It is how they work. Openshaw even felt sorry for him, pulling at the heartstrings regarding his alleged PTSD. I know as a sufferer of PTSD, what the darkness of the mind and the condition does to you, I can pretty much rule out PTSD in Duckenfield's case. It was or is a sympathy tool. Furthermore, if he was on a cocktail of antidepressants and large amounts of whisky, which was reported, his life chances would be very limited indeed.

Openshaw, amazingly, shockingly, described him as 'a poor chap'. It was obviously being played out, in a sea mist of bias, denial and corruption, of that there was no doubt. It was perfectly clear that a fit up, stitch up, call it what you will, was being orchestrated by Openshaw. What about fairness? Balance? And most of all, justice? It was not evident, from these out of touch judges, whether it was the disgraceful Stuart-Smith in 1997 with the judicial review, or Hooper and his show trial, at the private prosecutions in Leeds, in 2000, and again, in 2019 with Openshaw's Preston Crown Court debacle. I said Crown Court, what I should have said was *Clown* Court. For that, in essence, is what it was: a farce, straight out of a West End theatre.

In all seriousness, away from the dark humour, it was a totally heart-breaking, gut-wrenching time for all those who were affected by Hillsborough. How can anyone in their right mind not convict the accused who was charged with ninety-five counts of gross negligence manslaughter? It was not just one or two, it was almost 100, for goodness sake. I really would like to know who was on that jury. Yes, directions came from Openshaw, but do jurors not have their own minds? I have served on a Crown Court jury. You have to have balance, of course, be fair and without bias, and have some degree of intelligence, to separate fact from fiction. I sincerely doubt that those jurors had any sense of what was required of them. Quite simply, they were not up to the task. I will reiterate once more, that how can a jury give a verdict of not guilty in a criminal trial, when the inquest jury recorded a verdict of unlawfully killed and categorically stated that a charge of gross negligence manslaughter on ninety-five counts should be afforded in a Crown Court?

There was no basis for such a verdict. It was blindly obvious through hard evidence, witness statements, and even Duckenfield's glaring acceptance that he lied, and that he was not up to the job. It appeared that Duckenfield, through Masonic connections, could not be convicted. It was like a tube of cheap glue: nothing sticking.

Naturally, the families were heartbroken, ripped apart, overwhelmingly tearful, inconsolable, angry, frustrated.

Stop the press…

Sadly and shockingly, it does not end there. Only a mere few weeks later, the other defendants, Donald Denton and Allan Foster, former senior officers within South Yorkshire Police, and the force solicitor, Peter Metcalf, had 'their day in court'. Another example of the absolute travesty of Hillsborough. Due to the Covid pandemic, it was held at the 'Nightingale Court' in the bowels of Salford's Lowry Theatre. Yet another theatrical playbook of farce and falsehood. The three defendants, Denton, Foster and Metcalf, were charged with perverting the course of justice. This related to police statements that were either changed, altered or redacted, following Hillsborough, some thirty-two years ago. They knew they were involved in this shady practice, and so did we. So, an open and shut case then? Not a chance, and not when you have a judge in the form of Justice William Davis, who said that, 'they have no case to answer'. They got off on a technicality. A convenient lie. A corrupt member of the judiciary, and corrupt members of South Yorkshire Police. The old pals act, with probable influence with the dodgy Freemasons. To rub even more salt into the already fatal wounds, you have defence barristers, like the odious Johnathan Goldberg QC, who shockingly and disgustingly stated, 'This puts to bed, once and for all, the myth that Hillsborough was a cover up.'

Absolutely vile and sickening. I have already written to the Bar Standards Authority, regarding his crass behaviour. Will these short-sighted people ever learn?

Now comes the ultimate and final nail in the coffin over Hillsborough. As of yesterday, 4th June 2021, it was reported by BBC News, that South Yorkshire Police and West Midlands Police, had agreed compensation pay-outs to 601 bereaved family members, and survivors, of Hillsborough. Can anyone believe this degrading and ultimately wicked decision, that is ultimately a slap in the face to those who suffered terribly, either through physical, emotional or psychological pain, following Hillsborough? Yet again, it was down to cover up and collusion, smears and lies, and another glaring and indisputable example of the biggest miscarriage of justice in the history of the British legal system.

Chapter Fifteen

Fighting for Life

A year before the disgraceful Duckenfield trials at Preston Crown Court, I became very seriously ill. I had a very long stint in hospital, some four months. I suffered through a long list of severe life-threatening and life-changing conditions. A lot of people, including those who cared for me, honestly did not think I would make it. I almost didn't. It was that serious. It all started in the September of 2018. It was like a minefield, trying to take everything in. Whether it was the ambulance taking me to hospital, the endless visits to ward after ward, being wired up, countless blood tests, scans and transfusions, basically unable to go anywhere, confined to a bed for what seemed like forever, the endless monotony and boredom, and most importantly, no football, no Anfield, no Kop.

On my first visit to Royal Blackburn Hospital, I was diagnosed with lymphedema and cellulitis, when my legs swelled up like balloons, and I became incredibly breathless, to the point of needing oxygen. I was told I had to stay in and 'undergo investigations'. My legs, quite honestly, became a mess. Then I developed sepsis. Anyone who has ever had sepsis, knows full well it is a potential life-ending condition. The doctors and nurses could not figure out what was causing my developing illness. I was weak, tired, and always cold and shivery.

When it eventually came down to it, a superb consultant called Doctor Solomon, who was a kidney specialist, figured out I had a kidney injury. My kidneys were not working to full capacity, partly due to medication I had taken for a number of years. Without question, Doctor Solomon saved my life. However, hospital politics came to the fore and some doctors refused to believe it, arguing amongst themselves about my condition. That was one of the main reasons I was in there for so long. Now I have to say this, there were some wonderful doctors and nurses in that hospital. They did everything for me and were extremely compassionate and kind. I struck up a deep rapport with a few of the nursing staff, especially when I was confined to my own room. I was just a bit disappointed that I never got a bed bath!

Sadly, there were a few that were just not up to the job. There was minimum compassion and not much in the way of care. However, I was looked after well by so many wonderful people, whether they were consultants, doctors, nurses, domestics, paramedics or physios. I truly cannot thank them enough. They really did save my life.

I did an awful lot of thinking in that hospital bed. I certainly had one of those 'Road to Damascus' moments. I looked deeply into my own mortality, that certainly happens when you are so close to death. I have had many dark moments in my life. I had this complex 'freak show' inside my conflicted head for far too long. A lot of it revolved around PTSD and Hillsborough. I needed to get rid of the excess baggage and the horrible garbage. To cheat death, twice in your lifetime, certainly makes you focus. To bring much needed positivity into your life, really is an awesome feeling. In my own honest assessment, gone are the negatives, the heavy drinking, poor physical health, life not going anywhere. This has now been replaced by a healthy and nutritious diet, regular healthy exercise and abstinence. It changed me completely.

Chapter Sixteen

Breaking the Chain of Life: Goodnight and God Bless, Mum

Genevieve Whittle
24th November 1927—5th March 2020

When I was in hospital, from 2018-19, I had to take into account the immense stress that enveloped me that involved my late mum's illness. I cared for her for a number of years, as she battled dementia. Anyone who has been a carer for someone with this terrible condition, will know exactly what your life is like. There is little time for yourself, all the intense pressure is on you. It is a constant struggle, an uphill battle, being there 24/7 in an intense workload of cooking, cleaning, washing, bathing, countless hospital and doctors' appointments, and not to mention the abuse and rage given to you by your loved one. It wears you out, physically, emotionally, psychologically. The fact that I was stuck in hospital, unable to care for my mum, was a deeply distressing state to be in. Having to let my wife take the fall, with daily visits to hospital, looking after my mum, as well as her own very busy and stressful job as a nurse in a care home, was really too much for her. She dealt with it but at what cost? I really am lucky to have Deborah, first and foremost as my wife, and also as a soul mate.

After I was finally released from hospital, following a further setback that involved a mild stroke, it was time to focus on my mum, once more. Often in life, fate delivers a blow. Yet, very rarely this happens in a positive way. This was one of those times. Deborah often worried about my recovery, stating that both us, meaning my mum and myself, could have passed away. We all knew my mum's health was deteriorating quite rapidly. Her dementia had worsened markedly. Yet, when she fell and fractured her hip, we thought that was the end. Amazingly, my mum had her operation and came through it. She was ninety-two at that time, her fighting qualities were well known. We were warned by the hospital staff that the operation could take her to the grave; she may not respond. After some rehabilitation, in a smaller hospital, she was transferred to a familiar place: Dove Court in Burnley, where my late dad stayed for his final days in 2013. We were conscious of the fact my mum would have very little time left. I was recovering well, and I walked down to Dove Court almost every day. I was getting stronger. The family would have one final Christmas with my mum.

My mum, Genevieve Whittle, fell asleep on 6th March 2020. She was ninety-two years old. In conversations with our GP, the death certificate would say that the cause of death was dementia. Yet, we were informed that the cause of death could possibly be through Covid, as we were in the first phase of the virus. I guess we will never know. What really got to me was the fact we could not organise a proper funeral. My mum was a strong, devout Roman Catholic, and would have wanted a Requiem Mass in church. Sadly, it was not to be. A simple service at the crematorium, with just myself, Deborah and my daughter (stepdaughter) Kendra, in attendance. We felt it would be better if Monica, our beloved granddaughter, did not go to the service. Monica always called my mum GG (or great grandma). They loved each other to bits.

As I write this, we still haven't been able to take Mum's ashes to a special place, due to Covid. When the time is right, we will perform that task. My late father's ashes were scattered on the beach at Saint Annes on Sea, on the Lancashire coast. My late mother will soon be reunited with her loving husband of some sixty-two years. As a family, we always adored Saint Annes. It holds a special place in our hearts.

I can readily say that all three members of our family will be together again, in that better place they call Heaven. The chain of life may have been broken, until the day that I see them all again in paradise.

God bless you, Mum, Dad and Anthony. Your light shines bright and beaming. It is never dim and will never go out. YNWA.

Chapter Seventeen

A Nest of Vipers

More than thirty years on since the worst sporting disaster in British history, I still struggle to come to terms with what happened that day. It will never leave me. Moreover, the absolute fact that *nobody* has ever been held accountable, or has even made a full and frank apology that was heartfelt and sincere, is sickening, unjust and deplorable. The hurt that was inflicted on the families and survivors is nothing short of pure evil. The killing of 97 innocent men, women and children is a truly horrific crime. That is exactly what it was: a crime. A crime that had many willing participants, a lot of complex issues that were hidden, swept away, controlled. The deliberate abuse of power manifested itself in that crime.

As time has gone on, the numbers of those families and survivors have started to dwindle. Some have passed away well before their time. Some could not live with themselves. Some simply died of a broken heart. Some have grown old but still remember. The terrible consequences of Hillsborough still resonate today. A patchwork quilt of despair and raw emotion. Nothing to cling onto. Nothing but emptiness. Nothing but tears. Nothing.

Then you have a nest of vipers. That is the name I have given to this chapter. Directly or indirectly, that nest is full. The vipers are many and swarm and slither in their own lies. They will do absolutely anything to get their own way. To break the law, to smear, to collude, to lie, to fabricate, is their own personal badge of honour, or I should *say dishonour*. Whether they are police officers, journalists, media moguls, judges, barristers, writers, politicians, doctors, nurses, paramedics, church ministers, social workers, football authorities, safety providers et al. Their goal is the same: to win at all costs, no matter who they hurt along the way. The massive link of corruption around Hillsborough is deep, and far-reaching. A maze of dishonesty. It came from the very top right to the bottom.

The starting point was the tragedy itself, and Duckenfield's catastrophic failings, compounded by his blatant, cowardly lie. Then came his conversation with Graham Kelly and Glen Kirton of the FA. They were sucked in by it all, no questioning of 'maybe you were wrong'. This was then passed on to John Motson, the BBC football commentator, who 'had a line' about what happened, stating that 'fans without tickets broke through a gate to get in'. This came from Duckenfield's own mouth. Whilst people were dying, or fighting to save their own lives and indeed became heroes in the rescue, this vicious cancer of falsehood and fabrication went on unabated. The chaotic scene on the pitch, which now resembled a battlefield of carnage and confusion, was the most horrific example of death that I have ever witnessed. You simply do not get over such horrors. As all of this transpired, many police officers stood idly by, or formed a cordon so as not to let Liverpool fans get to the Forest supporters at the other end of the stadium. What reality were they in? What planet were they on? All that the Liverpool fans wanted to do was to save lives, using advertising hoardings as makeshift stretchers. Or to find friends or loved ones, and those who were deeply traumatised, like myself, were shaken and rattled in a daze, not knowing what to do or where to go. Yes, there were some police officers who bravely helped in the rescue, or tried to save tangled bodies, or gave the kiss of life. However, there were those who did nothing or simply lied. The fact that a senior police officer who stood outside the stadium with some forty ambulances lying idle, stated: 'You can't go inside, they're still fighting.'

A typical statement that was wholly untrue, but was their mindset in dealing with this avoidable disaster. A lie follows a lie, followed by another lie. So, it went on.

The police control box was another issue that needs addressing fully. We all know that Duckenfield dithered and delayed, before lying to the FA, inside the control box. Also, there was Assistant Chief Constable Walter Jackson, second only in authority to the chief constable himself. Someone with such a high rank, undoubtedly with a lot of experience, should surely have taken control of the situation. So, what did he do? Amazingly, Jackson cowered nervously under a desk, like a small child.

The next piece of evidence surrounds the TV monitors that Duckenfield lied about once again, insisting that they were not working. He used that falsehood to claim he could not see clearly towards the central pens (pens 3 and 4). Unfortunately, for Duckenfield, they had a very experienced TV technician on duty that afternoon in Roger Houldsworth. He proved they were working. Another lie. Furthermore, in total and utter desperation, there was a 'mysterious break-in' at the very same control box, on the night of 15th April 1989, as the horrific identification process was taking place in the club gymnasium, at the other end of the stadium. So, what was taken? A video tape, showing detailed footage filmed that very afternoon. So, who would take such a thing? For what purpose? I think that any right-minded individual should know the answer to that question. One final footnote to the whole control box saga is that Roger Houldsworth was not called to give evidence to the original flawed inquests in Sheffield. No surprise there then.

The following day, Sunday 16th April 1989, all the VIPs arrived. A who's who of the most contemptible, arrogant, lying, corrupt sewer rats ever to walk this earth. If you think of Hitler, Himmler and the SS, a fair description of people with similar virtues would be Thatcher, Ingham and the rest of the cohorts involved in one of the worst days in British history. They were all there, undoubtedly to plot and scheme, lie and collude and pass the blame. They stood on that horrific terrace of Leppings Lane, the broken barrier in the distance. Did they reflect? No. Were they bothered? No. Were they to blame? Absolutely yes. In their own way, they were all at fault.

Margaret Thatcher

She hated football, not to mention our great city of Liverpool even more. The fact that Thatcher had just decided to bring in a football ID card scheme, coupled with the scenario that she was thankful with South Yorkshire Police in the way they 'helped' during the Miners' Strike, and that she would use influence to aid the cover up.

Bernard Ingham

I doubt whether you could get any lower than this loathsome individual with his callous 'tanked up mob' assertion, he still holds today. They even despise him in his hometown of Hebden Bridge in West Yorkshire. After much public pressure, he was removed from a local newspaper, such was the outrage. He was Thatcher's press secretary in 1989.

Irving Patnick

A former Tory MP from Sheffield Hallam. His vile lies would make even Pinocchio look squeamish. He was responsible for vicious newspaper headlines, after contacting Whites News Agency in Sheffield, who in turn contacted The S*n rag.

Paul Middup

What a horrible, nasty, vile human being. He was the Police Federation spokesman in Sheffield. His lie-ridden verbal assault in the media, condemning Liverpool fans to disgusting slurs and myths has never been forgiven, nor forgotten. Seeing him on national TV news and blatantly lying through his teeth, claiming that 'you had to be drunk or mad to behave like that'. He continued his barrage over the coming days, weeks, months and even years. He now keeps a very low profile, due to the fact he was finally found out.

Douglas Hurd

Hurd was the Home Secretary at the time. He ordered for the Taylor Report to be established. Although not a willing participant, Hurd was still part of the cover up.

Graham Mackrell

I thought that was a small oily fish! Yet, not as oily as this insignificant little toad, and former club secretary at Sheffield Wednesday. The *only* one convicted at Preston Crown Court, albeit with a pathetic fine of a meagre £6,000. He even had the audacity to plead poverty, when he played a part in the deaths of 97 men, women and children. Shockingly, he *never* apologised.

Peter Wright

The former chief constable of South Yorkshire Police. It was under his command that Duckenfield got the job of match commander. Moreover, Wright was 'confident that his officers would be exonerated of any wrongdoing over Hillsborough'.

David Duckenfield

What can you say about this man, who ultimately cost the lives of 97 people on a sunny April day in Sheffield? To be termed as a gutless coward would be being kind. How about liar or corruptive? Then there is weak and leaderless, incompetent or dishonest.

There is nothing that can describe Duckenfield in any good light. A man who used his influence, with an abuse of power as a tool, with his own illicit connections to the Freemasons, literally got away with murder. Someone who dodged two Crown Court trials, a private prosecution and one flawed inquest. Someone who, despite being recorded as having an unlawfully killed and gross negligence manslaughter inquest verdict against his name, simply walked free. And you call that justice?

Norman Bettison

And then there was this man…

There are absolutely no redeeming qualities regarding this vile individual. He was part of the cover up over Hillsborough, leading a team of 'black ops' officers to 're-write' Hillsborough. There were secretive meetings in Sheffield pubs to 'create a story' over Hillsborough. Bettison climbed up the greasy pole to promotion, and became chief constable for two forces: West Yorkshire remembered with not great fondness, and shockingly, beforehand, with Merseyside Police. I can tell you, that did not go down well with the good people of Liverpool. He was appointed as chief constable of Merseyside, by none other than the Home Secretary, Jack Straw. You really could not make it up, could you?

Then, more sickening still, Bettison was knighted. Unbelievable. There were moves to have the knighthood expunged, through political pressure and petitions, but sadly, without success. One final footnote on Bettison. He even had the audacity and arrogance to 'write' a 'book' about Hillsborough. Naturally, it was 'ghost written' by one of those meaningless right-wing scribes. To be fair, Bettison has been successful in his fictional and fantasy writing.

These were the main culprits of a crime against humanity, decency and respect. A crime that was disgracefully and elaborately covered up to suit their own ends.

A shocking exposé of corruption, fabrication, falsehood, smears, myths, collusion and coercion.

There were others involved in this deep dereliction of duty. The media coverage of Hillsborough was controversial in its depiction of the tragedy. Naturally, the right-wing media was at the forefront of the unfounded and awful attacks on the victims, the survivors and most shocking of all, the 97 themselves. Even local newspapers weighed in, most notably The Sheffield Star and The Manchester Evening News. Yet, the most hideous, vile, disgraceful, shocking and disgusting coverage came in that purveyor of 'fake news', The S*n. The lurid, yet smear-led, wholly untruthful piece of gutter journalism, led by that unpalatable editor, Kelvin Mackenzie, who went in feet first with unsubstantiated allegations and blatant lies, and that now infamous and shocking headline, 'The Truth'. The fact was Mackenzie wanted to go with an even more brutal headline, 'You Scum'. Shocking. Yet, the subheadings were even more sickeningly callous and vile. The phrases 'fans beat up brave cops' or 'fans robbed the dead' or 'they urinated on corpses' were printed with intense vigour. All were absolute lies. Moreover, this was proved, many years down the line.

If you look deeper into the whole issue of Hillsborough, the right-wing press, Murdoch and Thatcher, you can find out what really did transpire. The indisputable fact was that Murdoch supported the Tories. The media baron, a very wealthy one, bank-rolled Thatcher. In return, certain favours were put in place. The Canary Wharf episode was one, as was crushing the unions. The highly paid boys in blue, thugs in uniform, Thatcher's police state, could basically do what they wanted, without any comebacks. The Miners' Strike of 1984-85 was, as I have already mentioned in a previous chapter, pivotal in Thatcher's destruction of the socialist left, the so-called 'enemy from within'. The vicious assault at Orgreave was central to the abuse of police powers. This came back to the surface four years later at Hillsborough. The role of South Yorkshire Police again came into question. The links were blindly obvious: Thatcher—Murdoch—the Tories—The S*n—South Yorkshire Police—Hillsborough. The fact that Mackenzie was merely a willing puppet, albeit an obnoxious one, just adds to the conspiracy.

If you look into the role of South Yorkshire Police, you will clearly see that the whole organisation was rotten to the core. This went from the very top in order of command. From the chief constable to assistant chief constables, to superintendents to inspectors, to sergeants, even to very keen PCs. It was all part of the structure. Undoubtedly, after Hillsborough, the closing of ranks and secretive meetings, involved other organisations and professions. The link between law and order and the medical profession stopped firmly at the door of the South Yorkshire coroner, the odious Stefan Popper. It is plainly obvious that a very tight knit group, run under the strictest of guidelines, operated with absolutely no feeling or empathy. This included policemen, lawyers, judges, solicitors, doctors, nurses, paramedics, pathologists, social workers and the clergy. It was devoid of human emotion. The emphasis was on a callous and clinical setting, ignoring the needs of those desperately wanting some kind of reassurance and support. Namely, the bereaved families or survivors. It was cold, unwelcoming, structured and harsh. Whether it was the youth club on Hammerton Road where relatives were told to gather, or the two main hospitals, the Northern General and the Royal Hallamshire, and even to the club gymnasium at Hillsborough, for the awful identification process. Then there was the soulless, cold, clinical Medico-Legal Centre in Sheffield. It was damning. It was diabolical. It was horrific.

Yes, there were some caring individuals who went out of their way to show kindness, compassion, care and reassurance. I applaud and salute them for that example of decency and dignity. The role of everyday, down to earth, yet generous Sheffielders, is often overlooked that day. Simply, they were magnificent. Whether to offer comfort, prepare food and drink, or merely being able to telephone home to say that you were safe, it really touched the heart. My own personal story is just one of many. I was deeply traumatised, unable to control or focus on my own emotions, shaking inside, shivering outside. I really could not speak, if I did, I just broke down in floods of tears. Like many others, I just walked away from the hell of Hillsborough and headed up Halifax Road and past Wadsley Bridge Station. There were some fans who were obviously shaken up as they could not locate their friend. It makes you wonder, what if?

The lovely couple who took me in were genuinely concerned about my health, both physical and psychological. I knew my ribs and chest hurt like hell. That very night, when I returned home, there was no chance of sleep, the trauma was overwhelming. My upper body was just one massive and extensive bruise. The cracked and bruised ribs were another indication that I was extremely lucky to be alive. It was also reassuring that this wonderful couple really felt for me. It was like I had been carried on angels' wings. They gave me sweet tea to aid the severe shock. I telephoned home and spoke to my mum. I just broke down uncontrollably. I will never, ever forget the beautiful people who cared for me. They were special. Beyond special. All that I can say is thank you. You'll never walk alone.

The difference was very stark, between those who helped me, and the authorities who did nothing. Angels with wings or a nest of vipers? I certainly know where I would rather be.

Chapter Eighteen

PTSD: A Personal Journey

To suffer from PTSD, or post-traumatic stress disorder, is something which I could not wish on anyone. It is truly horrible, a complex darkness that never seems to go away. Of course, the classic symptoms of PTSD, such as nightmares/night terrors, flashbacks, panic attacks, deep anger, pent up frustration, low self-esteem, lack of confidence, severe paranoia, screaming, crying, waking up in a cold sweat etc. is something which is not only frightening, but it is horrifically real. There is no escape, and has the potential to go on for many years. An inner darkness, where you face equally dark demons, your life being controlled in many variants. An escape into a world of drugs, alcohol or other vices. There is no sense of reality, even wallowing into a world of split personalities and deep mistrust.

You are then condemned, with most people not understanding your psychological pain. The usual criticisms come to the fore, such as 'get over it' or 'pull yourself together' and 'it's been going on for years'. The shocking accusations of 'self-pity bashing', or 'there is no sympathy here' is the uniform 'slagging off' mentality out there. Furthermore, there are those who say that 'PTSD is fake, it's not a real illness'. Sorry to shatter your illusions, but it most certainly is.

It has to be said that PTSD has many forms. There is military PTSD, PTSD through abuse, sexual PTSD, criminal PTSD and non-combat PTSD. The latter is the one that I would like to focus on, and the one that affects me. To survive a disaster, any disaster, is quite profound. It is like being in a war zone, but as a civilian you are not trained to cope with such horrors. It is bad enough to witness death in whatever professional role you undertake, but as a member of the public, you are not expected to be a victim. This is hugely forgotten, and disaster survivors are often not in the front of people's minds. Now I am not saying that disaster survivors are special, or they are better than other PTSD sufferers. Absolutely not. Anybody who has witnessed horrific trauma, in whatever circumstances, deserves my full respect and understanding. PTSD is a relatively new phenomenon, certainly in some people's opinion, and in certain ways it is challenged by several psychiatrists and counsellors. Yet, if you look at clinical research and with a historical mindset, you will find that a form of PTSD was recognised in Ancient Greece. In the First World War, deserters were routinely shot on the grounds of cowardice. In reality, serving soldiers were suffering from 'shellshock'. Of course, we now know it as PTSD. With the use of modern technology, as well as ground breaking research and education, this can only be of benefit to sufferers and mental health professionals alike.

To suffer from PTSD for more than thirty years, gives me some kind of knowledge and hindsight into the condition. The indisputable fact was that for almost twenty years, I had no support with PTSD whatsoever. As I have already mentioned in previous chapters, the first five and a half years from 1989 to 1994, that involved the horrors of both Hillsborough and my brother's tragic death, were the worst hell imaginable and my darkest days. A downward spiral, fuelled by alcohol, trying to exist whilst battling the symptoms of PTSD, that inner darkness that I have frequently talked about. There was a certain degree of morbidity in my life. Desperately trying to live a 'normal life' was a virtually impossible task. Whether it was work, relationships, interests or friendship. I routinely developed a very annoying habit of 'screwing things up'. Naturally, it was my condition of mental illness, not me, the person. Yet, I put the blame on myself, squarely at my door. A door that I often bolted and closed to the outside world. I much preferred a reclusive outlook on life at times. The wallowing in self-pity just did not resonate with me. Clearly, it should have done. At this current point in my life, I have the tools to recognise where I went wrong, to be brutally honest; such a focus is sometimes the only way to achieve.

Some ten years ago, I finally summoned up enough courage to try to get some psychological help with my PTSD. I pretty much knew I had the condition, but felt I needed an official diagnosis. After all, I had all the symptoms which I touched upon earlier. I had witnessed a deeply traumatic event, Hillsborough, as well as the tragic loss of my brother, Anthony. I looked at several options. First of all, I contacted my GP, who advised me to go along to a counselling session, which at that time was located at the surgery. I made an appointment to see a counsellor. Her name was Gail, and she was wonderful and very understanding. She recognised straight away, 'You have PTSD.'

That lifted a huge weight off my mind. It was like I had been held down by a huge rock, and that I was drowning in this sea of mental illness. It was a great relief that I finally got that recognition. Unfortunately, Gail stated she was about to go on maternity leave and that a new counsellor would deal with appointments in the future. I was so sorry to see her go. In that one-hour long appointment, she had opened up my mind and gave me some realistic hope. Sadly, her replacement was not so forthcoming. A forgettable experience, so much so that I cannot remember his name. The empathy was practically zero. He kept continually suggesting that, 'You really do not have PTSD'. I kept telling myself, 'How the hell do you know? You weren't there.' I was deeply disappointed with that appointment, so much so I decided there and then that I would not be going back.

I was back where I started. Full circle. I decided to do some research about further mental health provision. I looked at a place called Gannow Lane Resource Centre in Burnley. I waited a few weeks before an appointment came through. I actually was given an appointment with a psychiatrist! There the good news ends. It was a waste of time. The old assertion: 'you do not have PTSD'. Then he really got under my skin. As I explained about Hillsborough, he got utterly confused.

'Wasn't that a fire?'

'No,' I stated, 'That was Bradford. Hillsborough. The human crush when 96 people lost their lives.'

He simply did not have a clue. The next sentence really got me agitated. It was one of those clenched fist and gritted teeth moments: 'Oh, the stampede.'

Stampede? That is what they said in 1989, when they decided to lie and pass on the blame to the victims. I corrected him in every way possible. I was getting angry by this point, almost to a rage. How the hell can a psychiatrist, a mental health professional, not know about Hillsborough? How could he not see what my problem was? How could he misdiagnose a case that was blatantly obvious to be PTSD? It was ripping me apart. I think that he could see I was extremely angry and obviously very disappointed. When I got home, I promptly wrote a very lengthy and scathing letter to Mental Health Services. I think they knew I was severely cheesed off! A few weeks later, I received a letter offering another appointment with a different psychiatrist. I have never looked back.

Let me tell you a little bit about this wonderful psychiatrist. His name is Doctor Christopher Owumuchi, and besides sharing a brilliant first name, we both have a love of football. Sadly, he is an Arsenal fan but I don't hold that against him! He was a very tall African, and very cheery, as well as outgoing. He put me at ease straight away. I was asked to write about my experiences surrounding Hillsborough, and the state of my mental health. He could not have been more different. I felt very reassured, totally positive and incredibly thankful. It was decided that I would be given medication: 150 mg of sertraline per day. I call them my 'magic pills'. Personally, I have never looked back. Added to this, I received ground breaking EMDR counselling which was another break-through moment. I had this brilliant therapist, called Mark. This source of counselling is really awe inspiring, and you are put at ease straight away. It certainly is very reflective, calming and comforting. It is like you are taken to another world, and the inner deepness is so very bene-ficial. So, I say thank you to the wonderful people at the Magdalene Project in Bacup, Lancashire.

As I write this now, at the end of June 2021, as I have celebrated my sixtieth birthday, I can be truly grateful, thankful and very, very lucky. I have been on one hell of a journey. I have almost lost my life, twice. I was very much part of Britain's worst sporting disaster, and one of the most horrific of all time. I have battled PTSD. I lost my brother through tragedy. I lost both my parents, through ill health, caring for both of them, and always being there. I very nearly died, just three years ago. How-ever, I turned my life around in a positive way, and have a very beautiful, funny, intelligent granddaughter, who I worship and adore.

I am the lucky one. Many are not, and I feel for them all. Now is the time to help others. I am in such a posi-tion to be able to do so. It is time to give something back.

Chapter Nineteen

Oh, I am a Liverpudlian and I Come from the Spion Kop

As I come towards the completion of this book, it gives me time to reflect. A time to digest. A time to recall. This last June, 24th, I celebrated my sixtieth birthday. The big six-oh. Where have all the years gone? I certainly can point to a number of mistakes along the way. Some misjudgements, failures and foolish behaviour. I have had a life well-lived, a road well-trodden, a wild, stormy and vicious sea, well-navigated to the port of that storm. However, without question, I have, despite my failings, been mentally resilient and strong. Within all the depths of despair, I have developed this kind of unbreakable resolve and quiet determination. I simply had to. Some may say that I am a fighter. Maybe. Maybe not. I'll let others be the judge of that.

I am very keen on history. I studied this amazing subject towards my degree. I have also developed my writing skills over the years. I honestly believe this second book is a massive improvement on the first. That is not me being arrogant, smug or big-headed, merely the truth. Of course, that is up to you, the readers, in deciding what you think.

I would like to guide you down that place they call memory lane. There are a lot of treasures there, as well as a few pitfalls. My family tree is an interesting one. I can readily trace it back to County Mayo, Ireland, and the family name of Corcoran. My grandfather, Henry or 'Harry' Corcoran was born in 1902 in Ormskirk Hospital. My great grandfather worked the docks, and settled in Kirkdale for a while, before moving to Ormskirk.

My grandfather was the one who educated me in being a Red. He took me to my first game when I was four years old, and as they say, the rest is history. I will always remember with great fondness, as we walked up the hill and past The King Harry. Then I was warned by Grandad Henry, 'Don't you ever go inside that proddy alehouse.' I think that was given in jest and with a handful of salt. After all, I have been to King Harry many times over the years.

That first magical moment has stayed with me forever. I still feel the magic today. I am, of course, talking about strolling down Back Rockfield Road, and viewing the incomparable magnificent edifice that is the Spion Kop. Quite simply, the greatest standing terrace in world football. Nothing came close, either in England or overseas. You can keep your Stretford End, The Shed (isn't that a famous stand at a Rugby Union ground?), The North Bank at Arsenal or the Holte End at Villa. You can definitely keep the Gwladys Street at Goodison, please do not get me started on that cabbage patch! Not even the Jungle at Parkhead can suffice. As I looked in awe on that Saturday afternoon in 1965, at the intimidating, very unique structure, it was one amazing feeling for a four-year-old to take in. Thus, the love affair with LFC was born, and is still going strong to this day.

The history of the Spion Kop is a very interesting one. Whereas there are a lot of grounds in England who have a structure with the very same name, there is only one that is famed throughout the world, that every football fan knows about and that has an atmosphere and camaraderie second to none. So where does the name 'Spion Kop' derive from? The origin is from South Africa, and the Afrikaan people and language. The meaning is relatively simple. Spion Kop means 'spying' and 'hill' or 'top'. The Battle of Spion Kop was often regarded as one of the fiercest and deeply bloody battles during the Boer War, which took place during 1900. The Boer War, or the South African War, which ran from 11th October 1899 to 31st May 1902, involved the British Army confronting the Afrikaan (Dutch speaking) Boers from the Orange Free State and the Transvaal. It is also referred to as the Second Boer War. The Battle of Spion Kop lasted just two days (23rd-24th January 1900) near the besieged city of Ladysmith. There were over 200 fatalities.

In honour of the battle and terrible losses, it was decided by a number of football clubs that, as a tribute, terraces at grounds would be called Spion Kop, usually large areas behind the goal which climbed steeply. There were such areas at Leeds United, Bradford City, both Sheffield clubs, Birmingham City, Coventry, Notts County and Tranmere Rovers. The Spion Kop was built in 1906, and a steel roof was added in 1928. The capacity of the Kop at that time was over 27,000.

At that very first game, my grandad took me into the old standing Paddock. I kept annoying him, saying, 'I want to go in there.' I pointed furiously towards the Kop. In all the years that I have been watching the Redmen, I have stood or sat in every part of the ground. Naturally, the majority of times it has been in the Kop, but I had an affinity to the Paddock, being so close to the pitch and to view the Kop and the resplendent colour of red. I had a few visits to the Anny Road End, when it was expected to get a bit tasty and spicy, and rucks were going to develop. I have sat in the old Kemlyn Road Stand, and then the Centenary Stand, both lower and upper. I have even sat in the old Main Stand, or as I christened it, the Grandads' Stand!

I have a short and humorous story to tell. It was at one of the famed European nights. I was walking around the ground, taking in the Anfield air and soaking up the atmosphere. I heard this one strong voice, 'You got tickets? Anyone need tickets? Tickets…' It was obviously a tout trying to make a few bob. I think it was a game against Eastern European opposition if I remember correctly, possibly the crack Bulgarian outfit, CSKA Sofia in 1981. The tout then bellowed out, 'Tickets. I got tickets for the Kremlin Road!' You really cannot beat that wonderful Scouse humour. As it transpired, another Anfield glory night, and a 5-1 victory.

I have seen some many wonderful and weird things when watching Liverpool. At times, it would be pure comedy gold. I have also seen some amazingly gifted players in brilliant Liverpool sides. I have enjoyed the craic more times than I can remember. The pre-game buzz, the expectancy, the bevy, lots of bevy. The many friendships. The love, the companionship and, of course, the elation and the ecstasy. There are certain things that remind me. Getting the train to Ormskirk, then onto Kirkdale. The pub route to the ground. Those familiar names: The Peacock, The Abbey, The Stanley (later to become The Sportsman, run by Ronnie Whelan), The Elm Tree, The Pacific et al.

Of course, the pubs around the ground were very much frequented, such as The Albert, The Park and The Salisbury (now The Twelfth Man). There are certain things that remind you of those days. There was the drinking of Higsons ale in paper cups, pies and sausage rolls, needing a leak in the tightly packed Kop, and being extra careful so as not to spill some down an unfortunate Kopite's leg! Then there was the smell of beery piss rising up in a cloud of steam towards the top. There was the getting to the chinkies opposite the Kop for your curry and chips, before getting into the ground, just about in time for 'You'll Never Walk Alone'. Great memories that will be etched with joy and pleasure in the memory bank. After the game, usually with a thumping win, it was back to Kirkdale station, a few bevvies in the nearest hostelry, before catching the 6 p.m. train to Ormskirk.

The 1970s, and especially the 1980s, was a potentially dangerous time to be a football fan. It was the height of hooliganism. To be part of that era, in reality, putting your life at risk, was not only a serious danger to your health, but in a perverse way it gave you a kind of buzz, an adrenaline filled edge. The modern day football fan probably does not have much of a clue as regards to those days. The notion of getting up at the crack of dawn, catching your train, not wearing any colours apart from a small badge, to avoid the bizzies at away games, so as not to be frog marched in whatever weather, standing in shitholes of away ends, many without a roof, was the reality of the football supporter's life. The holy grail, as it were, was finding a 'safe' bevy house in the town or city that you were visiting.

I did them all, or virtually all, back in the day. I loved the cup games, as you visited places you would not usually go to. I waited expectantly for the FA Cup 3rd round draw. In those days, the FA Cup really meant something, as did the League Cup. I never missed a Wembley occasion, whether it was a European Cup final, FA Cup final, League Cup or Charity Shield. I started that run in 1978, as a seventeen-year-old, right up to 1990. What days they were. Our second European Cup triumph, when The King grabbed the winner, four League Cups in a row, two all Merseyside Cup finals, clinching the double in 1986, and the emotional, tearful, yet ultimately joyful FA Cup final in 1989, a few short weeks after the horrors of Hillsborough. Not to mention countless Charity Shields. No wonder that Wembley was re-christened Anfield South!

I have been asked many times, what was your favourite ground to visit? Well, I can tell you which one it wasn't. It wasn't Millwall. What an awful experience that was. An absolute shithole of a ground, dilapidated terraces and sick, racist scum. I even got a brick in the back as a welcome gift! Naturally, there was no finding 'safe' pubs. Safe pubs and Millwall do not coexist. For once, I was more than happy to be escorted to the away end. At least I can say that I went to the Old Den, and lived.

Over the years, I have been to some truly awful grounds. Many were unfit for purpose. The state of British football was on life support, it was chronically sick. The customers, namely the football fans, were treated abysmally. Added to this was the role of some very nasty police forces, who could basically do whatever they wanted. Is it little wonder that fans behaved like they did? After all, if they treated us like filth, then maybe we might as well behave like filth. It was a time of rebellion, riot and revenge.

It really made me particularly sad that I descended into football hooliganism, albeit in a relatively minor way. Yet, I upset my parents doing those rather stupid and selfish things. Now that they have passed and gone to a better place, it hurts even more now. My first conviction was in 1983 at Coventry City, and the old Highfield Road ground. It was when we had probably our worst performance of that season, a 4-0 mauling at the hands of a poor side. I got bevvied up in the city centre, and moved on to pubs near the ground, culminating at The Mercer Arms, opposite the entrance. Does anyone remember that pub? I was a bit worse for wear before I entered the ground. Soon after the kick off, it all started. I was on my feet, gesturing and using, you might say, 'colourful sign language'. I screamed out expletives, along the lines of, 'Come on, you Coventry bastards, have a f***in' go.'

Within seconds, I was pulled out of the stand, arms up my back, and taken to a 'meat wagon' and locked up. I heard the roar of the crowd and knew instantly that Coventry had scored. I soon found out that some of their boys had been pulled. There were the usual threats with the predictable 'wait until you get to court' bullshit. Mostly though, it was banter. I ended up at Coventry Police Station, dumped in a cell for an hour or two. Luckily, there were some of our boys in there, so the Cov lads didn't start anything else. I was charged and released. I was done for breach of the peace, and got a late train home. Now I had to face my parents…

I was back in Coventry a few weeks later, and an appearance in the magistrate's court. I could not help but laugh after they read out the details of the offence, especially those words I bellowed, 'Come on, you Coventry bastards, have a f***in' go.' I was slapped with a sixty quid fine.

The other offences I was charged with included urinating in a public place, twice. Once on Smethwick Rolfe Street Station after a game at West Brom, and the other in Blackburn, outside a pub in the town centre following a home game at Anfield. I was totally shit faced and decided it was a good idea to piss on a police car. Well, it seemed like a good idea at the time!

My final court appearance came in 1985. I had been at another Liverpool home game. I did my usual routine, Kirkdale to Ormskirk, then train to Preston. The guard collared me for smashing a lightbulb. He then promptly called for the British Transport Police at Preston station. I was arrested, then released. Around three months later, I was in court again, charged with criminal damage. The chief magistrate was a glum faced, miserable-looking git. I got the feeling he wanted to make an example of me.

My knees almost gave way when he stated, 'Given your growing reputation and number of convictions, we are seriously considering a custodial sentence.'

What the...? That was my wake-up call, my last conviction and my last appearance in court. That was in 1985, some thirty-seven years ago. I think that I have learnt my lesson, don't you?

I mentioned earlier in this chapter about my favourite grounds. If you remember, I stated how much I looked forward to the Cup ties. Such weird and wonderful places like Carlisle, Brentford, Stockport, Southend, Torquay et al. However, the one shining light above all others was York City. A drinker's paradise with a pub virtually on every street corner. We played there in the FA Cup, twice in the mid-eighties, at their tiny Bootham Crescent ground on the outskirts of the city. They gave us a good game, twice forcing replays. The ground was full to the brim, some 8,000 in attendance. It was a pleasant enough experience, and we were housed in the Grosvenor End, an open terrace behind the goal. It was a twenty-minute walk to/from York Railway Station. There was a good turnout amongst Lancashire Reds. I later found out that it kicked off with a series of rucks in the city centre, involving some York and Leeds fans, and the Redmen crew. Typical Leeds, trying to make a statement against a big rival. Well, you know what they say, sticking your nose in makes your face run red. I heard it kicked off by the River Ouse, around the bridge and in a number of boozers. Probably a case of lots of handbags and a little bravado.

Another favourite away trip was Watford, who had a brilliant side during the 1980s. I went down to London many times in those days. It was affordable back then, cheap prices at games, and a unique ticketing system on the train, you might say. A trip to Vicarage Road was a must, and the many pubs, most notably The One Crown, was an absolute necessity. It was all a bit different at Watford. They were not stained by hooliganism, probably the friendliest supporters in the country. I can vouch for that, meeting lovely, wonderful people, usually in The One Crown. It was certainly the highlight of the season.

I went to all the London grounds: Arsenal, Chelsea, QPR, Spurs, Millwall, Palace, Wimbledon, Charlton et al. The only ones that I ever missed were West Ham and Fulham. We never played Fulham, apart from the odd Cup tie, and West Ham, due to terrible bad luck, illness, bad weather, and the like. It was always on my bucket list.

It was not just London. Of course, all the north west grounds: Manchester City, United, Blackburn, Burnley, Preston, Bury, Wigan, Tranmere. I went to Sheffield (both Wednesday and United), Leeds, Bradford, Derby County, Nottingham Forest, Notts County, Leicester City, Stoke, Aston Villa, Birmingham City, Coventry City, Wolves, West Brom, Walsall, Newcastle, Sunderland, Middlesbrough, Carlisle, Oxford, Norwich, Ipswich, Luton, Southampton. Quite a list. If I was to look back, I would say that the worst three grounds I ever went to were Oxford United, Luton Town and Southampton. All three were small, tight, compact little grounds with small capacities. They also had high steel fences, and as an away fan you were treated to appalling conditions, penned in like sardines, in what was nothing more than cages. It beggars belief that we actually let them treat us like we did. They, being the football authorities and the police, were perfectly happy to herd us like cattle, treat us like third class citizens and subject us to horrendous treatment. They knew we would not complain. Maybe, looking back, we should have kicked up a fuss and demanded change. Would they have listened? Probably not. If they had, we would never have had the shocking tragedies of Bradford and Hillsborough.

Chapter Twenty

Looking Forward to the Future

As I write this, we are in the mid-early months of 2022. So, what does the future hold? At the moment, not very much. We are still in this global pandemic. Covid has taken so many lives around the world, young or old. It has been a hellish nightmare of self-imposed isolation, fear, severe anxiety, an NHS struggling to cope and Bungling Boris not in control of the situation, and the undoubted manipulation of double standards and gross hypocrisy. The unhelpful degree of the abuse of police powers, a startling return to Thatcher's police state. It seems like hell has returned. Having to isolate for over a year does affect your mental health and wellbeing. Thankfully, I have had a lot of time looking after my granddaughter, Monica, which admittedly, has kept me sane. The rumours that she drove me mad are a gross exaggeration!

I am frankly amazed, shocked, surprised that I have not contracted this awful virus. I thought that I would be a prime candidate given the health issues I have had to negotiate over the past couple of years. Yet, nothing at all, not even a sniffle. Must be stronger and more resilient than I ever imagined. The mechanism must now be at a level that helps me fight infections. I cannot be any luckier than that. I have come to the conclusion that I have finally realised my health is the most important part of my life. As I hit sixty, it is a page in my life where I cannot turn back. The best thing that I could possibly take from all of this is the fact I am damned lucky to be alive, that I cheated death, not once, but twice. Now that is possibly the most precious gift on the tree of life. I have my home, my family, my health and my faith. I have my love of LFC. I have the talents that Our Blessed Lord gave to me. I can finally say I am able to control and negotiate the turmoil of PTSD. I can say I have battled and beaten those demons. I can say I binned all of that garbage and negativity. I can finally say my life is not controlled by alcohol. Or by anger and resentment. I am clean in many different ways. I am positive. I am me. I am the new, freshly inspired me.

This book is dedicated to the 97 men, women and children who were so horrifically and brutally killed at Hillsborough on 15th April 1989. May they rest as angels in Our Lord's beautiful and majestic Kingdom.

For the heroic, bereaved families of the 97 and the gallant survivors of that day. Time to find peace and solitude and know they are safe in the knowledge that they proved without a shadow of a doubt that those at fault lied.

Whilst the law, in its corrupt practices, made sure of a cover up in their own court, and convictions of unlawfully killed and gross negligence manslaughter were cruelly ignored and were wiped away, be comforted by the law in Our Lord's court. Where judgement will be swift and truthful.

To those who portrayed a myth and sickening lies for over thirty years, whether they were prime ministers, governments, political aides, media barons, journalists, police and emergency services, the judiciary or other interested parties, be assured that God's justice will be given fairly but firmly.

To those who have fallen asleep in Christ, and suffered the pain of Hillsborough, as relatives or survivors, be comforted in the glory of the Heavenly Kingdom.

And to my family, who have departed this life to join in the glory of God in His Heavenly Kingdom. Christ's loving hand and His beautiful sacred heart will bless you in all the days of Heaven.

To my wonderful parents, Robert and Genevieve Whittle, to my brother, Anthony, free at last away from his tortured mind. To all the aunties and uncles, and especially my grandparents, who nurtured me.

And to Paul, my father-in-law, a true servant of Christ.

All be blessed by my love and prayers. Amen.

Andrew Devine

The 97th Hillsborough Angel

I have added this addition to the book following the passing away of Andrew Devine, taking the loss of life at Hillsborough to 97. The 97 Angels. To survive for more than thirty-two years, when the 'medical professionals' had decided he would not last very long, shows you not only the true spirit and resolve of this remarkable man, but also highlights the wrongful assumptions of those in charge, or the so called 'experts'.

Remember the crass opinions of the coroner, Stefan Popper, who falsely claimed in the original flawed inquests that: 'Those that died did so by 3:15 p.m.'?

This kind of blows that ship out of the water, even more so. We all know that there were many victims 'with the potential to live'.

Yet, Andrew Devine survived, not just for a few hours, or even days, or months, but for thirty-two years. That, without doubt, points to a very special individual with immense courage, fortitude, desire and an incredible iron will.

Sleep well, Andrew. Goodnight and God bless.
YNWA. GBNF.

Other Sporting Heroes

I am a sporting buff. Obviously, football is my number one passion. However, I do watch other sports on television, especially the famous global events such as the Olympics, and some much closer to home, like Wimbledon, the Open, Test Match Cricket et al. I have an affiliation with several sporting icons, who were legends in their own time.

Sir Ian Botham

This was in an era when cricket was king. I can remember warm sunny days, watching the test match on the BBC, with a perfectly ice cold lager. Heaven. I have always been a fan of 'Beefy' aka Ian Botham. He was a maverick, some may say a flawed genius. To me, he was an entertainer, and the fact he was at odds with who he described as 'gin slinging old dodderers' makes him even greater in my eyes. The upper class toffs of Eton and Harrow, so out of touch with the real world, simply did not approve of the great man. They had this futile assumption of what an Englishman should be like, and how he should behave. It is all well and good at the Long Room, or the Members' Pavilion at Lords, but I say bollocks to all of that.

His finest hour as a cricketer was undoubtedly the Ashes series in 1981. Everything seemed lost, Beefy was horribly out of form, after he was sacked as England captain by the 'snobby dodderers'. The Aussies dominated and won the first test comfortably. The second test at Lords ended in a draw. The next game was on the Yorkshire side of the Pennines. The third test was staged at Headingley in Leeds. It was one of those iconic great sporting moments that we live for.

On the face of it, it pointed to another Aussie victory. It was the only possible outcome, but two men had other ideas: Ian Botham and the late, great Bob Willis. The England backs were well and truly against the wall. Even if England batted again, the total would be small and be easily gettable. There was some glimmer of hope in the first innings, as Beefy took 6-55 as he bowled and then hit a half century. In the second innings, wickets tumbled, defeat was almost inevitable. Botham was still at the crease, and was joined by the tail enders, Dilley, Old and Willis. The idea was to push the score along and get to at least a modest score. Yet, the brilliance of Botham, where he smashed 149 not out all over Headingley, at least gave the bowlers something to bowl at. The total meant that Australia just needed 130 to win. When they were at 56-1, seemingly it was an impossible task.

Yet, good captains make key decisions. Mike Brearley was such a captain. Not overly blessed with batting talent, he was the one who kept things calm, quiet and reassuring. It is fair to say Brearley was not the type to smash a quickfire century. He was a bit of a plodder, certainly not a risk taker. Methodical was his way. However, he was an absolutely brilliant captain. A ponderous thinker. Brearley decided he wanted to change at which end Bob Willis bowled from. It was a masterstroke. It meant Willis could use the slope to his advantage and claimed figures of 8-43. Australia were bowled out for 111, often seen as a score that brings bad luck. The one thing that you can say is that the Aussies never really recovered from that test match.

The fourth test at Edgbaston, Birmingham was another close affair, but when Botham ripped through the Aussies, in the second innings, with unbelievable figures of 6-11 it was a case of game over. The momentum was with England now.

The fifth test at Old Trafford (at the cricket ground, not that other place down the road) was one of those moments of sporting folklore. Another blistering Beefy century of 118, who some believe was his greatest ever innings, was the highlight of the test. It also meant that the Ashes had been won by 3-1, with only the final Oval test to come. Traditionally, the final test, especially at the Oval, usually ends up as a draw. And so, it proved. An Ashes series like no other. A team written off, a former captain in poor form, the Aussies dominant. Yet, this was the Ashes. This was Botham's Ashes. A true sporting icon.

The Calypso Kings and Somerset

In the height of summer, I watched some cricket, not just on TV. I enjoyed the Sunday League encounters that were forty overs per side, at Old Trafford, on a few occasions. I enjoyed local league cricket too. The memories of Whalley CC, running the bar and paid in pints, enjoying the banter and good laughs with the players, were wonderful times, of which I have a huge fondness.

As cricket teams go, however, my love was for the West Indies and Somerset County Cricket Club. In my humble opinion, the Windies were the best cricketing nation in the world, and in their pomp, did not lose a test series for fifteen years. Somerset were simply the greatest one day side throughout the 1980s. They were there to entertain, simple as that. Furthermore, they had the three cricketing Gods, in Vivian Richards, Ian Botham and Joel Garner. Magnificent!

Bjorn Borg

When you think about Sweden, you automatically remember the days of ABBA, and unflattering Scandinavian cars. Then there is Ikea, of course. There is one name that stands out above all others: Bjorn Borg. Before this sporting icon came on the scene, who truly revolutionised the game of tennis, nobody could ever name any Swedish tennis player. Well, the Ice Borg changed all that. He first became noticed as a seventeen-year-old at Wimbledon, yet three years later, he won his first Men's Singles Title, despite being only twenty years of age. Borg went on to claim a total of five successive Wimbledon titles and six successive French Open wins.

A true measure of a tennis genius is someone who can dominate on clay and on grass. They are two very different surfaces; clay is slow, whereas grass is lightening quick. To master both is almost impossible. Yes, Federer has dominated on grass, but not clay. Nadal, by the same token, has dominated on clay, but is not so good on grass. There will be those who will claim that Federer and Nadal have won more Grand Slams. That might be true, but they have had many years to do it. The fact was Borg gave up the game in his mid-twenties. He could and would have won many more Grand Slams, but he decided to call it a day, not even at his peak. It is perfectly true that Bjorn Borg suffered severe burnout. He had decided that enough was enough.

The game of tennis has changed over the years, the modern game is almost totally reliant on power and brute force. The equipment, namely the racquet, is of titanium structure, and generates immense power. The old wooden racquet was a totally different scenario. You had to rely on skill, and to outwit your opponent. Remember the baseline rallies? It is now all serve and volley. It is plainly obvious that it was much harder in those golden days of tennis. Of course, we had the greatest ever Wimbledon Final of all time, the iconic Borg vs. McEnroe battle. The Iceman vs. The Superbrat. They were two totally different characters, with opposing philosophies. Amazingly, they were, and still are, very good friends. Those memorable days of the mid to late 70s were a joy to behold and watch on the BBC.

Olympic Sporting Icons

I have witnessed many Olympics, both summer and winter versions. There are a lot of treasured memories that I have in my memory bank. This list is almost exclusively British, with one or two exceptions. Every four years, just like the World Cup, the expectation is strong. A great time to be a sports fan. Whether it was Daley Thompson in his decathlon glory days or Sir Steve Redgrave with rowing for gold after gold. The long list of track and field athletes, cyclists, swimmers, hockey teams, even sailing is very much part of our long and decorated sporting history.

They say that politics and sport should not mix. Yet, sometimes it is unavoidable. The tit for tat expulsions between the USA and the USSR, at the height of the Cold War could have set off a dangerous precedent. Thankfully, it did not. The Olympic spirit still rings true, and that was never more appropriate than in the Olympic Winter Games of 1980, held in Lake Placid, USA. The hand of friendship was offered in the Olympic ice hockey semi-final, between the USA and the USSR. Often regarded as sworn enemies, they played a very physical and intense match that the Americans won 4-3. The USSR dominated Olympic ice hockey and held four gold medals in a row. They were considered unbeatable. Yet, the USA beat them. Their squad consisted of mainly amateur players and college students. There were no NHL superstars amongst their ranks. That made this feat even more remarkable. The USA won the gold in the final against Finland.

If you go back to early Olympic history, one Olympic Games stands out. I am talking about 1936 and Berlin, the games that were supposed to cement Nazi Germany's Aryan dominance, and prove their misguided and totally false interpretation of the superior master race. It did not quite work out that way, much to Hitler's annoyance and obvious irritation. When one man wins four gold medals, and is of coloured skin, that really does blow those theories clean out of the water. It is quite possible that the late Jesse Owens could arguably be regarded as the greatest Olympian of all time. Sadly, the racism was not just confined to Germany. The American Athletics Board, and under pressure from right-wing senators, were not altogether pleased that these great men of colour had triumphed. Those who were there at the Berlin games in 1936, were treated abysmally on their return and were unable to find significant employment. A disgusting footnote to all of this. It is absolutely true to say that things never change and sadly, they possibly never will.

Poetic Words of Tribute

Why?

Why did it take nearly 30 years?
Why did it take so many?
Why did they lie and smear?
Why did they blame the blameless?
Why did we drown in a sea of tears?
Why?

Why were there no convictions?
Why did they never say sorry?
Why use the system in a callous way?
Why the heartache, fear and worry?
Why?

Why did the 97 lives mean nothing to you?
Why did you protect the guilty ones?
Why not in the public interest you said?
Why did you need to turn the screw?
Why?

Why all the judges, police and MPs?
Why all the journos selling a cold myth?
Why did the case cost millions of pounds?
Why?

Why all the bodies on a gymnasium floor?
Why choose that hell of the Hillsborough ground?
Why all the carnage, like a scene from a war?
Why? A simple question. Why?

Freak Show

The darkness that swallows your life
You face all this hell so brutal and real
No turning back, there is nothing to see
The glimpses of flashbacks
So, what else is new?
The obsession with death
Is still ringing true
This is my freak show
Do you know how I feel?

A wild animal, a cage, a public display
They look at me with no pity at all
What's there to see?
Just a freak show
That is my hell

I say 'help' but nobody hears
A head, a brick wall and nothing is done
Get over it, you are not really ill
How would you know?
Live my life, it's frighteningly real
This is my freak show
So simple and true.

Nothing Sticks

Do you have a pot of glue?
You see nothing works
Thirty plus years and solid fact
But hey, this is Duckenfield, you see
The Lodge held the answers
They always find a path to abuse
He killed 97 people
Sorry, there is nothing we can do

Nothing sticks, so you say
Trials, inquests and more
Unlawfully killed?
No, not even a sniff
We have judges, jurors and solicitors too,
      all part of the plot
That is how you turn the screw

So, it's off down to Dorset
No worries at all
A round of golf, a seaside retreat
How do you sleep?
Well, he doesn't toss or turn
Not with fake PTSD
You are right, nothing sticks
What else can we do?

Acknowledgements and Heartfelt Thanks

A lot of situations have transpired since the first book. As a family, we have suffered terrible loss, yet we have had some very happy occasions too. These include:

My Loving Mum and Dad

I cared for you both right up to the end. I have a lot to be grateful and thankful for. You had long and happy lives. Yet, there were times of tragedy, firstly, with me surviving Hillsborough and then my brother, Anthony, and his tragic death. We lost you in 1994. Yet, nothing was done. You passed away in terrible circumstances amidst the torture of severe mental illness. Now you have Mum and Dad to comfort you in Christ's Kingdom.

Paul, My Father-in-Law

A true servant of Christ. I remember the many years we shared our Roman Catholic faith. You supported us and helped us through many struggles. I am forever thankful for that.

Deborah, My Beautiful Wife

This world is full of some wonderful people. Yet, nothing or nobody compares to you. Your immense generosity, love, care, guidance, loyalty and humour. Your unwavering commitment and sacrifice has been truly awe-inspiring. I love and cherish you so much, my darling XXXXXXXXXX

Monica, My Little Princess

My beautiful granddaughter, Monica Rose, the day you came into my life, on 17th December 2013, was the greatest day of my life, a day that I will treasure forever. We have that deep and unbreakable bond that grandad and granddaughter have. It is special. You have also sat in the Kop with me, experiencing greatness.

I love you, Monica Moo.

Kendra and Ben

Kendra, it has taken a long time for me to focus on life and what it has entailed. Having PTSD for so many years, put a stranglehold on personal and family life. I did not do things that were right, I should not have treated you like I did. I should have reacted differently. I should have been a better parent. All that I can say now is I am deeply sorry.

Those words that are inscribed on your necklace that I gave to you as a Christmas gift, surely do run true.

You changed me.

That is absolute fact. I am so glad that you met Ben. He is a wonderful father to Monica. It shows. The turmoil of a few years ago has gone now. We had to all pull together. When you two finally get married, it will be a great family occasion. It will be the greatest time of Ben's life, but enough about the stag do! I love you, Kendra, as my own daughter. I am here for you no matter what.

Stop the press: they are now husband and wife!

Zachary and Jen

Zachary, I know we clashed a number of times over the years. It is not very surprising given that I have PTSD and you have Asperger's. It was bound to happen. Despite all of that, I really do care a lot about you. I am extremely happy that you found Jen. You are perfectly suited to each other.

I am pretty sure you will both have a wonderful life together. One slight complaint, why them?

Doris, My Mother-in-Law

I know I tease you with mother-in-law jokes straight out of the Les Dawson comedy bible, but it is clearly all in jest. Now I don't know if 'mother-in-law' is an anagram of 'woman Hitler'… only joking!

In all seriousness, it has been particularly hard for you after losing Paul. It is not easy. We have had a few losses over a number of years, and it has been very difficult, to say the least. However, I find some comfort in the fact that yourself and my mum shared the same birthday. God bless you, Doris.

All My Family and Friends

We have had good days, sad days, wonderful days and difficult days.

So, thank you to:

- Andrew, Rachael, Noah and Millie
- Anthony, Christine, Henry, Jack and Teddy
- Frances, Gary, Kate and Josh
- Angela, Bryan, Ella, Eva and George

And to everyone connected to our rapidly growing family!

The Health Professionals

Here is a list of those wonderful people who either saved my life or gave good service:

- Doctor Christopher Owemuchi: The brilliant psychiatrist who listened to me and diagnosed my condition of PTSD. He helped to change my outlook on life.
- Doctor Solomon: The consultant kidney specialist who sorted out my medication problems and diagnosed a kidney injury.
- The Stroke Team, Royal Blackburn Hospital: All the doctors, nurses and support staff who were truly magnificent with me after a stroke.

A *big* thank you to all medical staff in various wards and departments who got me through a very difficult time in my life. A special mention to Lisa, the trolley dolly!

And finally…

The Beautiful 97 Angels
JFT97 ♥ YNWA

Epilogue

Return to Leppings Lane

As I have gotten much older, maybe wiser (possibly), I tend to reflect more deeply on many things. Naturally, Hillsborough is my main concern.

A few weeks ago, I took my eight-year-old granddaughter to Hillsborough, for the very first time. She has asked everything there is ask regarding Hillsborough. Given the recent so-called 'death mocking' slurs and smears, it is perfectly clear that education is key. How do these people justify these crass and diabolical actions? The fact is, they cannot. That is why the brilliant proposal of Ian Byrne MP, a fellow Hillsborough survivor, to try to place Hillsborough on the national curriculum, and formulate a Hillsborough Day, around the anniversary of 15th April within the school year is crucial. His monumental 'The Real Truth Legacy Project' is fundamental in regards to education and learning and *must* be fully adopted.

When Monica and myself travelled to Hillsborough, it was a difficult task undoubtedly. Yet, to have my Monica Moo there was an immense comfort. We lay bunches of flowers around what was Pen 4 just below the tunnel. The steep tunnel is still there and the 6:1 gradient is eerily recognisable, though some alterations have been made. We walked along the pitch; the first time I have done so since 15th April 1989, when I was ripped to shreds and an emotional mess.

We saw the area where the heroic fans tried to save lives. We saw the area where the former club gymnasium was housed, and was part of the sickening and inhumane identification process with the callous shouts of, 'the body belongs to the coroner of South Yorkshire, not you.' The shocking process of wild accusations all part of the fit up. We saw the former police control box, where Duckenfield dithered, delayed and ultimately lied. We saw the inner and outer concourses. We saw what was once Gate C and that Duckenfield lie. The very scenes of the biggest sporting disaster in British history. What culminated in the biggest single miscarriage of justice in the history of the British legal system.

JFT97 ♥ YNWA
The bereaved families
The gallant survivors
The beautiful 97 angels
And all who have left us in the past thirty-three years

Heartfelt thanks to Trevor Braithwaite and SWFC for offering the support and understanding during our visit. It was much appreciated.

The Outer Concourse at Hillsborough and the infamous Leppings Lane end.

The tunnel at Leppings Lane, leading to the central pens 3 & 4 which cost 97 innocent lives, left many injured and thousands traumatised. Note the steep 6:1 gradient of that tunnel.

The Police Control Box was situated here. The current box is new and updated. The original one was an old, wooden structure, yet still had a clear view of those pens. This is where Duckenfield 'froze' and dithered and delayed and ultimately lied through his teeth.

The area around where the old club gymnasium was situated. This was where the callous identification process of the dead took place, and the vile questioning and interrogation of grief stricken loved ones and the insistence of the repeatedly wicked assertion that 'THE BODY IS THE PROPERTY OF THE CORONER OF SOUTH YORKSHIRE, NOT YOU.'

A new exit gate similar to the one that was finally opened to relieve the pressure outside—the now infamous GATE C—in which Duckenfield blatantly lied about and claimed about, in his words, 'DRUNKEN FANS WITHOUT TICKETS BROKE IT DOWN TO GET IN.'

We all know the REAL TRUTH.

Again, the Outer Concourse of Leppings Lane. Even today, some 33 years on, you can still get a sense of the tight and very tense, bottleneck that caused much fear and pain. If you notice the large steel railings, beyond that was the fast flowing River Don. If you look to the far end there is another large gate which was, and still is, a dead end.

Burnley General Hospital where I was treated on the night of the 15th of April 1989. The worst night imaginable.

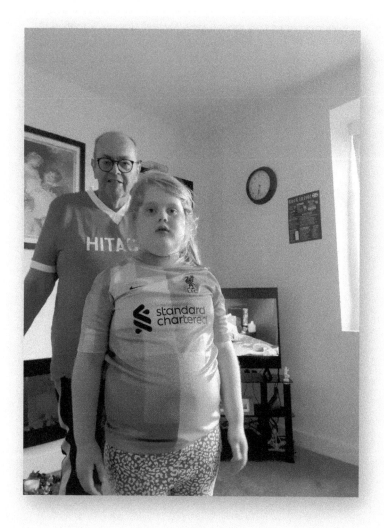

Myself and my beautiful granddaughter Monica. True Reds for life.

My (step)daughter's Wedding Day, Kendra with her husband, Ben, and of course, Monica!!!

My JUSTICE FOR THE 97 flag, often displayed in my back garden.

The beautiful water gardens at St Anne's on Sea on the Lancashire Coast. My late parents loved this special place for many, many years.

The St Anne's Water Gardens a place for quiet reflection and peace.

Dove Court Nursing Home where both of my parents spent their final few days of life.

The beach at St Anne's where both of my parents' ashes are scattered.
A fitting tribute.

Another memorable St Anne's vista.

Lightning Source UK Ltd.
Milton Keynes UK
UKHW010210061122
411729UK00001B/38